TRANSFORMING THE CITY

TRANSFORMING THE CITY

Reframing Education for Urban Ministry

Eldin Villafañe,
Bruce W. Jackson,
Robert A. Evans,
Alice Frazer Evans

WILLIAM B. EERDMANS PUBLISHING COMPANY
GRAND RAPIDS, MICHIGAN / CAMBRIDGE, U.K.

Wm. B. Eerdmans Publishing Co.
255 Jefferson Ave. S.E., Grand Rapids, Michigan 49503 /
P.O. Box 163, Cambridge CB3 9PU U.K.

Printed in the United States of America

07 06 05 04 03 02   7 6 5 4 3 2 1

Library of Congress Cataloging-in-Publication Data

Transforming the city: reframing education for urban ministry /
Eldin Villafañe . . . [et al.].
p.   cm.
Includes bibliographical references.
ISBN 0-8028-4968-7 (pbk.: alk. paper)
1. City clergy — Training of — United States — Case studies.
2. Theology — Study and teaching — United States — Case Studies.
I. Villafañe, Eldin, 1940-

BV637.5.R44 2002
230'.07 1'173 — dc21

2001053856

www.eerdmans.com

For G. Douglass Lewis

Disciplined developer of transforming education
for urban ministry and devoted disciple of
peacemaking and peacebuilding

Chairman, Board of Directors, Plowshares Institute
(1981-   )
President, Wesley Theological Seminary
(1982-2002)

"Blessed are the peacemakers,
for they will be called the children of God."
Matthew 5:9 NRSV

Contents

CONTENTS

Contents

CONTENTS

Preface

ROBERT M. FRANKLIN

"The saving of our world . . . will come not through the complacent adjustment of the conforming majority, but through the creative maladjustment of a nonconforming minority."[1]

MARTIN LUTHER KING, JR.

This is a very exciting time for people of faith, transformed nonconformists, who seek to improve the quality of life in our cities. Consider the recent evidence. The Charitable Choice clause of federal welfare reform legislation authorizes state and local governments to provide direct financial support to religious institutions that deliver secular social services. A growing number of national and community foundations provide support to religious organizations that serve the common good. Secular not-for-profit agencies that have expertise and resources for relieving urban misery are beginning to explore how they might collaborate with communities of faith. And, most exciting of all, a new cadre of clergy and lay people have emerged who understand the inseparable relationship between personal spirituality and social responsibility. The time is ripe for bold and creative urban ministries. Such ministries, to be effective, must work at many complementary lev-

1. Martin Luther King, *Strength to Love* (Cleveland, Ohio: William Collins & World Publishing Co., 1986), p. 23.

els and will require special leaders who are the products of a special kind of formation and educational process.

Let me begin with an observation about the varieties of urban ministries. I would suggest that at least five zones of urban ministry are discernible today. The most elementary level of urban ministry is commonly described as the *ministry of charity and mercy,* which provides direct and immediate relief to people who suffer. Fortunately, most congregations are involved in providing immediate responses to people who are hungry, homeless, or in need of medical care or money for transportation. *Ministries of nurture* and sustained support seek to enable people to become self-reliant and capable of securing employment, caring for their children, and maintaining a household. This demands a greater commitment of time and resources than the ministry of charity and mercy. Third is the *ministry of human service delivery,* which involves an institutional commitment to providing services to the public. This includes ministries such as child care, after-school services, literacy tutoring, job training, and so on. Often, these ministries are subsidized by philanthropic or government agencies. According to *Independent Sector,* a Washington-based private research agency, six out of ten congregations provide human services that benefit the larger public. These first three zones of ministry are fortified by the *ministry of justice,* better known as prophetic, public witness and activism. This work represents the needs of the least advantaged members of the society before corporate, government, and other powers that have the capacity to improve or diminish their lives. Among the agencies involved in this work are the public ministry of the U.S. Council of Catholic Bishops, the National Council of the Churches of Christ, Sojourners, and the Congress of National Black Churches. Justice ministries not only operate at the level of representation and rhetoric, but they seek to transform and redistribute both wealth and power. This is the ministry that advances the unfinished agenda of Dr. King's "beloved community." Fifth, the *ministry of comprehensive community transformation* finds churches taking the lead in developing and announcing a vision of the good community and the good city. When and where they are able, churches should play a leading role in acquiring vacant land, organizing capital for development purposes, incubating microenterprises and appropriate entrepreneurial initiatives, and using the wealth of the church to facilitate job creation and access to credit while promoting environmentally respectful development practices. Some of the voices you will encounter in this volume bear witness to the hopeful and redemptive models of community building by skilled urban ministries.

Leaders who engage the city in these and many other ways must be formed and nurtured. Transformed nonconformists do not appear automatically or accidentally. At best, such leaders emerge from learning contexts that have been forged in the flame of experimentation, evaluation, prayer, and practical, critical, and theological thinking. Strategic theological thinking and planning about urban ministry should give some attention to matters of curriculum, faculty, institutional partnership, evaluation, and the warrants (biblical, theological, and ethical) for such ministry.

Curriculum is a critical element in shaping women and men for more effective urban ministry. For me, the question that lies at the heart of the curriculum issue is not so much which courses students should take but rather, "What is the conversation that students must join in order to be competent in this arena of ministry?" What questions are being asked and addressed? What resources, data, and analytic methods are they relying on? What must be known before speaking and acting and even praying responsibly for the city? And, what is the end or purpose that the conversation seeks to advance? Warren Dennis reminds us of one important purpose of the conversation, namely, bridging the space that separates the cultures of the academy, the church, and the community or public. I regard the space that separates these entities as unredeemed but potentially sacred space — where a lurking revelation and insight await our willingness to breach traditions in favor of dialogue, collaboration, and mutual understanding.

Some person or group must guide the conversation. Unguided conversations may miss critical learning opportunities. This is a role for the gifted people known as the faculty. Rebutting an old adage to the contrary, an anonymous observer has commented that "those who can, teach. Those who can't, go into some less significant line of work." But the label "faculty" suggests that only people with doctoral degrees and tweed jackets need respond. Not so. In fact, it might be better to speak of such conversation guides as *"lead teachers,"* to borrow a phrase from Carl Dudley. Within that group will be seminary professors, local pastors, not-for-profit agency staff, government officials, grassroots community activists, young people who teach from their experience and testimonies, and each of the peers in the conversation. The essays in this volume suggest a broader definition of faculty and teacher.

That said, we must not let traditional seminary faculty and administrators off the hook. Mary Hennessey's essay reminds us of those tragic instances wherein the academic guild avoids excessive contact with practical theologians and practitioners of urban ministry, even when those practitioners sponsor innovative and effective training venues. Despite their effectiveness, they can't be real colleagues because they don't wear tweed or read our journal articles or attend our guild meetings. In order to positively transform the way that we form leaders for urban ministry, smart and passionate people from every level and sector of church leadership development must join the conversation. A book like this one can help to inform that conversation.

Perhaps it is time for all of us who care about faith in the city to pay closer attention to the quality of training programs at all levels, from accredited graduate seminary instruction to community- and congregation-based models. How effective is the seminary's continuing education program in retooling current pastors for the evolving urban context? It is also important to ensure that people from outside the familiar conversation circle are invited to assist us in being as honest and self-critical as possible. Imagine convening a meeting to examine and evaluate the current shape of your urban ministry program. In addition to the lead teachers and students, you also invite a local police officer, a barber, a journalist, a homeless shelter resident, and a teenager. Wouldn't that make for a more sparkling, and perhaps, productive conversation? No guarantee, of course, but I think the spirit of Pentecost prompts church leaders to celebrate when people from differing stations in life can speak the same truth in their own local tongues.

This leads us to the importance of strategic *institutional partnerships*. Former Surgeon General Dr. Jocelyn Elders once defined collaboration as "an unnatural act between two non-consenting adults." That certainly underscores the difficulty of the art of collaboration. But collaborate we must. The seminary and the church cannot prepare leaders for urban ministry only in hermetically sealed monasteries. We do not have sufficient resources, or information, or credibility to do so. We need friends — conversation partners. When I was a member of the Ford Foundation staff, we talked often of trying to promote unlikely partnerships between organizations that had expertise in certain arenas but might benefit from collaborating with others. We need people who understand the city, its politics, its economic infrastructure, its various cultures, its changing demographics, and its future prospects to be in dialogue with those who are the custodians of the city's memory, conscience, and values. Theologians must be part of the dialogue about the future of cities, all cities. We must want to join that conversation, and we must insist upon room at the table.

Business gurus consistently report that evaluation is the most important ongoing activity that makes for dynamic, effective, leading organizations. Evaluation informs us of our unfinished agenda and lets us know what our future learning curve must address. Seminary and church leaders who are honest will admit that urban ministry is not a very high priority on most agendas. Unfortunately, many people regard better worship, a greater emphasis on personal spirituality, and healing ministries as being of greater relevance to their lives. Although this is understandable, this popular demand threatens to distort Christ's intent (our mission) in a broken world. Let us remember that we have been anointed and commissioned to proclaim and practice God's reign on the earth.

Cities are places to which people are drawn by the irresistible promise of an exciting life characterized by a plurality of choices for crafting their lives and making meaning. But cities are also places of chaos, oppression, alienation, loneliness, and despair. They are sinful places, or, at least, places where sin comfortably resides. Consequently, God's people need to inhabit the public square, and God's word must be heard in the marketplace of ideas and life options. Thus, spirituality, liturgy, and therapy are neither inimical to, nor competitors with, urban ministry in the church's action agenda. Indeed, all of these have a rightful place in an effective urban witness for the church.

Finally, Ray Bakke reminds us that the Bible begins in a garden but ends in a city. God loves the idea of the city. And God loves actual gritty, grimy cities with all of their ordered chaos and possibility. Extraordinary, even magical things happen in places that offer so much stimulation, choice, and safe harbor to strangers. Perhaps this points to another reason why Jesus and all of the Hebrew prophets were so drawn to Jerusalem.

In January 1999, I had the honor of co-leading a delegation of twelve Christian seminary presidents and deans to Israel. Rabbi Jim

PREFACE

Rudin of the American Jewish Committee was our primary guide and co-leader. After an exhausting plane trip, we boarded a small bus en route to downtown Jerusalem. Still some distance from the city, the bus stopped suddenly along the roadside. Rabbi Rudin urged us to disembark. Huddled together in the cold evening, staring out at a city bathed in the distant light, he read Psalm 122:6 in the Hebrew language. "Pray for the peace of Jerusalem, and that all will go well for those who love her."

As I listened to those intriguing words, I also whispered a silent prayer. I thought of all the transformed nonconformists throughout the world working for the shalom of their cities. I thought of the frustration that accompanies ministry in the city. For despite all of the work and prayer of Christians, Jews, and Muslims Jerusalem still is not a city of peace. Nor is your hometown.

But we are not free to cease our prayers and good deeds. As Cornel West reminds us, we are captives of hope. We believe that the final act in the divine/human drama has not yet been played. And we may yet participate in completing that script. So, as the church of Christ, we choose, audaciously but humbly, not to despair or dismay over the transitions and turpitude of the city. Rather, we are bold to share our testimonies of how the Holy Spirit still works through inconspicuous acts of grace and goodness and justice, ever transforming those mysterious and promising urban places where so many of us live and move and have our being. This book is such a testimony — stories, models, and wisdom about how we should and may place urban ministry among our highest priorities.

Atlanta, Georgia

I. INTRODUCTION

Invitation to Dialogue

"He who has never traveled thinks his mother is the only cook."

WEST AFRICAN PROVERB

"Professor, what do you mean when you say we interpret Scripture through the lens of our lives? Last week you emphasized that exegesis is the process of finding out what a passage meant to the original hearers and then discovering how the text applies to our own time. Now, it sounds like you are saying something different."

Professor Kingsdale-Ortiz replied, "Not really. No matter how hard we try, we do not come to a biblical passage or even ministry without presuppositions. Our prior experiences shape the way we view life, which affects our understanding of life. For instance, those of you doing urban ministry who have lived in a city for your entire life — before someone told you, did you think there might be different perspectives on how ministry is done? Probably not. We tend to view life as urban people, and unless we meet someone who doesn't share that perspective, we might never realize the differences."

If Professor Kingsdale-Ortiz is correct in her assertion that our frames of experience shape how we view life, what does this mean for preparing people for urban ministry? How does our framework affect what we do and how we do it? How do the ways we view ministry in the city shape how we prepare people for that specific ministry?

Questions abound; answers are much more difficult to come by.

One thing is clear — experience is teaching us that the traditional or classical approaches to education do not work well in the ever-changing climate of the city. The dynamic and complex nature of our cities demands that we begin to think differently about the nature of urban ministry and how we develop leaders. An important skill in community mediation is to recast the problem so it is more open to mutual, beneficial resolutions. This is called reframing. We need to reframe our current thinking and thus our actions in education for urban ministry.

This book does not pretend to have all the answers. We don't even claim to know all of the questions that are at issue. However, we do sense that what is needed is a new way to look at urban ministry training and, thus, how to prepare for and engage effectively in this ministry. A tool for reframing is to present case studies of six very different examples of urban theological education as a vehicle to raise questions about the nature of leadership development. These chapters are more of an invitation to an ongoing dialogue than a neatly packaged series of answers.

Why use case studies? Why not propose how to do urban ministry and train others to do it as well? The authors are convinced of the power of story or narrative as a critical vehicle for teaching and learning. All of the following cases are grounded in historical reality, and the issues raised in them are born out of concrete experience. However, they can serve to explore issues and themes raised in the reader's experience as well. The cases have the attraction and power of true engaging mystery. Each has a plot, characters, and a problem. However, the last chapter is missing; to "complete" the story calls for your engagement and commitment.

Each of the six cases is a slice of life, a "snapshot" of events and people at a particular time and place. Readers and those discussing each case should be aware that since the time of these snapshots, there have been numerous changes in the context, programs, personnel, and the primary issues and challenges facing each of the institutions described here. This is normal and to be expected of living institutions. The names of the organizations and some historical figures involved in each case are given, but at the suggestion of the authors, and because of the ever-changing landscape of institutions, the names of the primary characters are disguised to protect their privacy. We are deeply indebted to the individuals and institutions that were willing to share their visions and some of the challenges of urban theological education in order to provide rich learning opportunities for their colleagues.

The particular type of case study we used is known as "problem-posing." The individuals and organizations faced crucial decisions. Information is given about the problem and the background leading up to the point of decision, but the reader is not told what happened after the point of decision. Such an arrangement leads the reader to a dialogue that is specific to his or her context. The discussion notes with each case will help those employing this resource to generate their own dialogue.

Emerging Frames for Understanding Urban Ministry

A frame around a piece of art serves to set off the painting from its background and focus attention on the artwork itself. A good frame complements the painting and does not detract from the image inside. In a conceptual manner, a frame allows one to put parameters around an object to distinguish it and to focus attention on the object of concern. The frame serves as a kind of lens, homing in on the subject in greater detail and analysis. The six frames that appear below derive from the authors' experience in urban ministry and dialogue with the cases and their commentators. These frames are not exhaustive, but they serve as starting points for how the authors view urban ministry in general and urban theological education in particular. In articulating these emerging frames, we consciously acknowledge that we are promoting an approach to urban ministry by suggesting that practitioners and theorists must wrestle with each of them. By doing this we are suggesting that when we talk about reframing education for urban ministry, we are aiming for changes in both thinking and acting. Changing our perceptions or our conceptual viewpoints is a portion of the picture. We want to challenge you to wrestle with new ways of acting, of doing urban ministry and education, based upon a "reframed" understanding. Our six frames of reference are described below.

Contextualization can be imaged theologically in the incarnation, where Christ, divesting himself of divine privilege, became human. Thus an urban theological education program is *situated*, both administratively and programmatically, in the context of ministry so that we have an "urban kenosis" — a self-emptying into the city. The theology, curriculum, teaching methods, academic policies, and administrative structures are informed by the context of ministry (that is, by the city and its constituencies). Structural contextualization implies that the costs, procedures, policies, and teaching methods are "fitted" to the context of service so as to maximize the delivery of theological education to as many people as possible. Contextualization is a commitment to the *shalom* of the city. This means that a program of theological education seeks to affirm the city as a locus of God's redemptive activity. Contextualization means that the gospel is seen holistically, addressing the personal and the social — for example, both evangelism *and* social justice.

Constituency addresses the fundamental questions of whom are we educating. Our assumption is that urban theological education is for the whole "people of God" and not just the clergy. The whole church must witness to the whole gospel through word and deed. Thus constituency addresses both in-service training for those already engaged in urban ministry and pre-service training for those who are preparing to enter ministry in urban settings. Constituency also addresses the multicultural dimensions of our cities, paying particular attention to the historic ethnic and minority groups in our cities, such as African Americans, Latinos, and European communities of Italian and Irish, as well as the recent immigrant groups such as Haitians, Brazilians, and Southeast Asians. A third factor of constituency encompasses gender. The role of women in urban ministry is a long and distinguished one; thus urban ministry programs must grapple with how to maximize inclusion. The whole body of Christ should be represented; thus its ecumenical thrust.

Community is defined by the relationship of programs to institutions, cultures, social fabric, and religious ethos. An urban ministry program must work closely in conjunction with its community, which transcends the individual students enrolled. The leadership, teachers, and staff of an urban ministry program, whenever possible, should be drawn from the community. They must be known and respected in the community and must maintain good relationships with other key leaders. The program must be "owned" by the community so that the churches and community feel that this is "our" program, even when there are no individual students from a particular church currently enrolled in the program. The program should "look" like its community and be sensitive to the community's assets as well as its perceived needs. Community implies educational cooperation with other existing urban organizations such as social service agencies as well as in other aspects of urban life.

Curriculum deals with the entire aspect of what is and is not taught and the manner in which it is communicated. Thus we are talking about the explicit curriculum — what we intend to teach; the implicit curriculum — unintended aspects such as the ethos or the manner something gets taught; and the null curriculum — that which is omitted entirely, either consciously or unconsciously. The curriculum must wrestle with the broader goals of theological education: to *form* church leaders among God's people; to *inform* them about their faith and its application to modern life; and to equip them to become agents of *transformation* in the churches, denominations, and communities where God has placed them. High on our understanding of curriculum is one that takes a pedagogical — or androgogical — approach that utilizes an action/reflection model of teaching. Concurrent with contextualization, the curriculum also addresses the question of excellence, which is not exclusively defined by the professional academic guilds, but also by the urban constituency and reality. It is a curriculum that wrestles with how to be in concert with the demand to integrate theory and practice in coursework and ministry.

Collaboration emphasizes the need for various institutions and programs to work together, recognizing a common sense of mission and purpose for doing theological education for urban ministry. Collaboration ideally should encompass as wide a spectrum of levels involved in theological education as possible. Thus Bible institutes, colleges, seminaries, and grassroots organizations should all work together toward the goal of educating the whole people of God. While collaborative partnerships do not have to be formal in a legal sense, though they can be, they should seek to approach a mutually affirmed and shared sense of equality in the relationship. In other words, all partners should feel they are getting as much as they are giving. By emphasizing the need for partnership among the various programs that are already doing urban theological education, cooperation instead of competition for scarce resources should be the result. Collaboration could be in such areas as shared curriculum, resource development and allocation, shared faculty and library resources, or joint programming. Creative structures might remain housed within one particular institution, or spun off to create a new nonprofit agency. The specific structure of each partnership is to be determined by the constituent members. Collaboration is the practical recognition that an individualistic approach to the city is unbiblical, unprofitable, and unproductive. The job is too large to squabble over issues of turf. Collaboration speaks of partnership. It goes beyond a client and network relationship to genuine sharing *(koinonia)*.

Confession (Spirituality) celebrates and affirms the rich distinctives of a program's theological and ecclesiastical history and emphasis. At the same time, there should be openness to a plurality of religious experience. For some this might include interreligious dialogue; others may not be able to be that pluralistic, but might still be able to affirm the larger traditions within the fabric of Christendom. Christians must come to theological terms with what it means not only to have a Jewish synagogue but also a Muslim mosque or Hindu temple in our urban centers. These believers are our city neighbors. Urban ministry programs face the dialectic that students come to the program in some sense with their spirituality already formed, yet in a continual open state, receptive for further development. In a very real sense, spirituality has both stable and ongoing dimensions to it, which should be interwoven throughout all aspects of the training, not just in one or two sets of courses. Urban ministry programs build upon the spirituality that exists in students, shaping it to become more nuanced and in tune with the urban reality. Spirituality speaks both to the personal and social dimensions of the students' religious journeys. It is both contemplative and apostolic.

The six cases have been placed into pairs of emerging frames: Contextualization and Constituency; Community and Curriculum; and Collaboration and Confession. By doing so we are not suggesting that the case studies in the community and curriculum cluster, for instance, have not wrestled with contextualization and constituency. You will find elements of all six frames in each case. However, we have grouped the cases according to those frames that seem to be the most relevant. In addition, numerous issues emerge as strong threads running through all six organizations. New York Theological Seminary, CUME, and CUTS are all wrestling with the parameters of mission as reflected in curriculum content. SCUPE, CUTS, and the Urban Institute, among others, face the challenge of sustaining non-traditional forms of urban education for ministry in a tradition-dominated establishment. Students and faculty at Haggard School of Theology, New York Theological Seminary, and CUTS deal with the ramifications of transforming teaching approaches to the urban context. The costs and benefits of the relations with partner institutions affect the basic fiber of all of the organizations presented. Our learning may come not only from dialogue about these issues, but also from considering the distinctive approaches each organization brings to this mission.

A Distinction between Examples and Models

You will notice that we have tried to avoid applying the term "model" to the cases. This is by design. Models are context-specific. On the other hand, examples are built upon principles, which are more generalizable insights that must be fitted to concrete historical situations. The problem with models, as instructive as they may be, is that they do not easily transplant from one specific context to another. Trying to do things the way a model does it usually results in frustration, producing feelings that the "model doesn't work." The institutions portrayed in these cases do exhibit various aspects of urban theological education, but you will immediately note that they are quite different from each other. They have in common, however, their attempt to deliver urban theological education in a faithful and responsive manner. Each one arose out of concrete historical contexts and continues to operate in them. We suggest that you explore the principles that underlie each case and then use these as springboards to consider your own specific ministerial context.

To provoke reframing our thinking and action in urban theological education, each case is followed by discussion notes that suggest ways it can be used to explore existing ministry practice, and each set of cases is accompanied by commentaries from distinguished urban ministry practitioners. We are convinced that these cases can and will be utilized effectively by people directly involved in urban theological education — students, professors, administrators, and trustees. However, because the nature and mission of the church in the city serve as a backdrop to many of the cases presented, this book can be used by those who are urgently concerned about the product of urban ministry education — persons who are recipients, not shapers of urban theological education. Several of the cases have already been piloted successfully with urban church laity to examine the mission of the church in the city. Thus, this book is also intended for denominational officials, pastors, and church leadership boards and committees who are seriously concerned about how to minister *and* continually prepare people for ministry in our urban centers. If we are to reframe how we view urban ministry preparation, we need to expand the dialogue. At the heart of this book is a passion to reframe and reform. So come, join us in dialogue.

How Did We Get Here? A Survey of Important Historical, Social, and Theological Issues That Occasioned the Rise of Urban Theological Education

BRUCE W. JACKSON

The six urban theological education programs presented as cases in this book did not arise out of a vacuum. There were forces and factors that helped shape their specific responses to the city. All are concerned with the vital question, "How do we train leaders to minister in the urban context?" In this essay, I will attempt to sketch what I see to be important issues that caused special programs for urban theological education to emerge. Elements of this survey will apply more to some cases than others, but I hope to draw together some of the main themes that are common to all of the cases.

Setting the Stage: A Brief Survey of Sociological Trends Affecting Urban Churches

Ministry in the city is not a new phenomenon. Clifford Green's book, *Churches, Cities, and Human Community: Urban Ministry in the United States 1945-1985,* provides a wealth of information regarding denominational responses to the challenge of urban ministry.[1] Indeed, for years the

1. See, for instance, Clifford J. Green, ed., *Churches, Cities, and Human Community: Urban Ministry in the United States 1945-1985* (Grand Rapids: Eerdmans, 1996), which details the issues that confront urban churches in such a way as to challenge

11

large, downtown urban church was considered to be the "plum" parish appointment, reserved only for the most experienced, dynamic, and educated ministers. Drive through the downtown of most major cities and you will see a myriad of "Old First" churches, regardless of their particular denominational affiliation. Some of these magnificent edifices still house vital congregations that have adapted with skill and verve to the dynamism of the urban environment. Others exist as shells of their former greatness, surviving as monuments to the past. Still others have closed their doors forever.

The flux of migration and immigration patterns is certainly a key reason why urban churches experienced rapid change in their ministries. In particular the migration of African Americans from the South to the North after the Civil War to around the 1960s deeply affected the dynamic of cities, particularly those in the north and northeast portions of the country.[2] Coupled with the many waves of immigration from places such as Ireland, Sweden, Poland, Eastern Europe, Germany, China, Japan, and Korea, this movement made our cities increasingly diverse, not only in ethnicity, but in terms of religious practice. Latinos from Puerto Rico and the Caribbean, as well as Central America, have affected the cities in the eastern portion of the country, while the south, central, and western cities have seen influxes from Mexico and Central America. More recently, immigrants from the Far East to Pacific Rim cities continue this ever-changing process.

A second key dynamic affecting the city and its churches was the phenomenon of suburbanization. In the 1950s, with the return of veter-

---

their continued existence. This work, by Green's own admission, is focused primarily on the responses of denominational church bodies to the changing urban scene. Green writes, "In the eighties and nineties, as many of the activities documented here were cut back, other initiatives began to appear, especially among evangelicals. That is a new stage that needs to be documented and analyzed" (p. ix).

2. David Halberstam eloquently describes the processes that pushed and pulled African Americans northward. They came to escape the oppressive, overt racism of the deep South as well as to seek the promise of a better future economically and, on the face of things, a more tolerant racial climate. See David Halberstam, *The Fifties* (New York: Villard Books, 1993), pp. 442-46. See also Luther E. Smith, Jr., "To Be Untrammeled and Free: The Urban Ministry Work of the CME Church: 1944-90," in Clifford J. Green, ed., *Churches, Cities, and Human Community,* pp. 54-56.

ans from World War II and the newfound prosperity of the growing middle class, the promise of home ownership began to draw ever-growing numbers of people, mostly whites, from our nation's cities. Sprawling housing developments such as Levittown emerged, almost overnight, fueled in part by the housing policies of the federal government. The onset of the development of the interstate highway system enabled Americans to work in the city and commute to their homes in the suburbs.[3] In the decade between 1950 and 1960, many cities in the Northeast found that their racial and socio-economic composition changed dramatically. "White flight" from the cities began in earnest. As whites moved out, others moved in. Space does not permit me to dwell on unscrupulous techniques such as block-busting or red-lining, but suffice it to say, there were forces that both pushed and pulled people to sell their homes and flee from their old neighborhoods to places surrounding our cities.[4]

The movement of people from the city (suburbanization), together with an influx of new people — immigrants and migrants, to a great extent persons of color — set the stage for the social upheaval of the 1960s and early 70s. Scenes on the evening news reinforced a growing perception that our inner cities were unsafe, crime-infested, unpleasant places to raise a family. Urban renewal in the late 1960s and early 70s resulted more in the removal of people from so-called slum areas than it did in renewal. Huge high-rise apartments to warehouse the poor — "The Projects" — quickly became a stereotype of the inner city.

Simultaneously, these demographic and social changes were accompanied by a changing economic system. The shift from a manufac-

---

3. Halberstam, pp. 131-43, describes the creation of the first Levittown in New York, and makes specific note (p. 141) that Blacks could not buy into the developments created by Levitt, a policy that would last two decades, long after the nation began to pass legislation banning racial discrimination.

4. For a clear and chilling description of the federal policies that helped to fuel the creation of suburban communities at the expense of the nation's inner cities, see Buzz Bissinger, *A Prayer for the City* (New York: Random House, 1997), pp. 203-12. Explaining the Home Owners Loan Corporation's practice of appraising communities to determine the suitability of lending, Bissinger claims that in almost every case, race and class determined the relative risk of each community. The cities, due to the nature of their housing stock and their tendency to be the first point of entry for migrants and immigrants, received the most devastating appraisals, a practice that came to be known as "red-lining."

turing base to service industries, which continues today, began during this era. The promises of a union-wage job and secure middle-class status suddenly were thrown into question. Mills and plants began to close, sporadically at first, but in ever-increasing numbers, forcing people to relocate or to move.

As the cities changed demographically, socially, and economically, the churches began to feel the pinch as members who used to flock to their services suddenly ceased to come.[5] Commuting to church, the perception that the inner city was increasingly dangerous, an aging church population, and changing neighborhood contexts contributed to declining church membership rolls. At the same time, existing suburban churches began to grow — some rather dramatically — as their communities grew. Denominations began to emphasize new church starts in the burgeoning suburban communities. These new churches began to accommodate the lifestyle of people who had moved to such areas. However, there was a lag in the institutional response of seminaries to the rapid urbanization of our world. Theological education for urban ministry, as a distinct field or discipline, is a relatively new phenomenon — perhaps only forty or so years old. I suggest the early 1960s as a logical starting date for urban theological education's emergence as a distinct field, in its nascent forms.

Attempts to Train Ministers for the Urban Scene: The Rise of Action Training

Immediately prior to the 1960s, theological education wrestled with its relevancy to the modern world. To paint the picture broadly, two camps emerged that framed the debate: those who emphasized academic preparation for ministry and those who stressed practical training. The view

5. See Harvie M. Conn, *The American City and the Evangelical Church: A Historical Overview* (Grand Rapids: Baker, 1994); William Julius Wilson, *The Truly Disadvantaged: The Inner City, the Underclass, and Public Policy* (Chicago: University of Chicago Press, 1987); and Theodore Walker, Jr., *Empower the People: Social Ethics for the African-American Church,* The Bishop Henry McNeal Turner Series in North American Black Religion, ed. James H. Cone, vol. 5 (Maryknoll, N.Y.: Orbis Books, 1991). All three note that American cities increasingly are two cities in one geographic area: the "haves" and the "have-nots."

of the minister as a "pastoral director," emphasizing training and equipping the church for ministry, gradually evolved into viewing the minister as a "professional" similar to a doctor or a lawyer. This paradigm shift affected the curriculum design of seminary education and resulted in the ever-increasing menu of courses designed to address the issue of relevancy.[6]

At the same time that seminaries were wrestling with the tensions produced by the acceptance of the professional education paradigm and reform in the seminary curriculum, churches were confronted by urbanization and questions of relevancy to the contemporary world. Many urban ministers began to sense that they were unprepared to face the challenges of the modern urban world. Their previous seminary training had not prepared them for the cataclysmic upheavals that the 1960s would bring. The 1960s and early 70s witnessed the rise of ethnic minorities demanding a redefined role in all of society's institutions, including theological schools. This, coupled with the flight of Anglos from the inner cities, resulted in a crisis for many of the older, white, mainline denominations.[7] Arthur Walmsley, an Episcopal Bishop in Connecticut with extensive urban experience, draws this conclusion when he writes that "the main-line, predominately white denominations in America began to face acutely their failure to penetrate the culture of an urban society."[8] Realizing that their survival in the city was at stake, these denomi-

6. Several major reports of a survey done in the 1950s resulted in three books: H. Richard Niebuhr, *The Purpose of the Church and Its Ministry* (New York: Harper & Brothers, 1956); H. Richard Niebuhr and Daniel Day Williams, eds., *The Ministry in Historical Perspectives* (New York: Harper and Row, 1956); and H. Richard Niebuhr, Daniel Day Williams, and James M. Gustafson, *The Advancement of Theological Education* (New York: Harper & Brothers, 1957). See Niebuhr et al., *Advancement of Theological Education*, p. 80. See also Edward Farley, *Theologia: The Fragmentation and Unity of Theological Education* (Philadelphia: Fortress Press, 1983), p. 109; and Robert Wood Lynn, "Notes Toward a History: Theological Encyclopedia and the Evolution of Protestant Seminary Curriculum, 1808-1868," *Theological Education* 17 (Spring 1981): 135.

7. See Gibson Winter, *The Suburban Captivity of the Churches* (Garden City, N.Y.: Doubleday, 1961); Gaylord B. Noyce, *The Responsible Suburban Church* (Philadelphia: Westminster Press, 1970); and Douglas C. McConnell, *Urban Ministries Training: Evaluating for Effectiveness* (Altadena, Calif.: Barnabas Resources, 1985).

8. Arthur E. Walmsley, "Action Training," in *New Occasions: Review of a Decade of Experimentation, 1961-1970*, ed. Executive Council of the Episcopal Church, Sec-

nations began to develop alternative methods, apart from the seminaries, to train ministers for the urban context. These programs became known as "action training." Action training was designed either to complement or to replace entirely the institutional seminary[9] and to address the need of the church to become more responsive to the challenges of urbanization.

Two of the best-known programs were the Urban Training Center for Christian Mission in Chicago, launched in 1963 after two years of discussion and planning by twelve denominations, and Metropolitan Urban Service Training (MUST), begun in 1965 in New York. Initially action training was geared for both laity and clergy, but the focus gravitated to the professional retraining of clergy. Action training was based on the assumption that the church could and should be a primary actor in the urban scene. Given the right sociological and theological tools to critically analyze reality, together with the correct structures, the church could positively impact modern society. However, these assumptions were challenged by the "emergence of militancy among Blacks and poor people . . . [which] set action training on a different course [than originally envisioned]."[10]

By 1968, a number of action training centers across the country had formed the Action Training Coalition. In June of that year, Robert Bonthius, spokesperson for the Coalition, presented a statement before the annual meeting of the American Association of Theological Schools. Offered as a response to the "Theological Curriculum for the 1970s," the paper presented the differences between seminary faculty and action trainers. He highlighted three issues: the meaning of secular involvement, the university or society as the center (context) for change, and the difference between doing theology and/or teaching it in the abstract. Bonthius maintained that the seminaries were unconcerned about their students' secular involvement, that they gravitated toward the university's emphasis on teaching and research, and that they taught theology in the abstract. In contrast, Bonthius argued that

tion for Experimental and Specialized Services (New York: Executive Council of the Episcopal Church, n.d.), p. 5.

9. George D. Younger, "Materials for a History of Action Training," n.d., 1-3-1-4.

10. Walmsley, "Action Training," pp. 5-7.

action training emphasized the need for students to be involved in the secular world in ways that were oriented toward change, not maintaining the status quo. Action trainers viewed the seminaries and universities as being too concerned with research and information transmittal and not concerned enough about social change. Finally, trainers were convinced that theology could not be taught abstractly; it had to be taught in the context of engaging a society that was in conflict.[11]

While action training began as a challenge to traditional theological education and its apparent unresponsiveness to urban society, it began to drift toward seminary renewal and cooperation and evolved into both a methodology and a theology.[12] There were three central theological presuppositions in action training: (1) action training placed an emphasis on action, activity, and doing; (2) action training viewed the minister as a facilitator of change within a shared church leadership; and (3) action training was a theological method concerned more with doing than with being.[13] Obviously, such statements only served to highlight the tension felt in the seminary community, where some objected to the emphasis on "doing" theology as opposed to studying it. This questioning of the underlying epistemology of traditional forms of theological education was part and parcel of the role that action training played in challenging the seminaries in the 1960s.

Action training as a movement had a rather short life, but its mark on theological education is clear. Action training influenced some of the programs described in the cases that follow, particularly New York Theological Seminary and the Seminary Consortium for Urban Theological Education (SCUPE). SCUPE students, for instance, are challenged during their experience in Chicago to engage in a critical analysis of urban systems, discerning structures and forces at work in the city. Building upon this analysis, they discover the role their church has to play in social transformation. Indeed, one student upon returning to his home seminary wanted to focus his thesis on his institution's complicity in tearing down the town's only homeless shelter!

11. Robert H. Bonthius, "Resources Planning in Theological Education: A Response and an Offer," *Theological Education* 5 (Winter 1969): 67-72.
12. Nathan Kollar, "Action Training: A Methodology and Theology," *Theological Education* 7 (Autumn 1970): 57.
13. Kollar, "Action Training: A Methodology and Theology," pp. 58-62.

Much of the enthusiasm and dialogue that occurred regarding action training never percolated down to mainstream clergy. It is interesting to note that the same liberal Protestant denominations that embraced this model of ministry subsequently experienced a dramatic collapse of their membership and societal influence. This leads one to question whether or not, at this period in time, the lifeblood of the church in the inner city had already begun to shift into other areas outside of the mainline denominations, perhaps into sectarian type congregations.[14] Action training was an attempt to reform seminary education, making it more responsive to the specific needs of the urban church and the challenges of urban society. It affected theological education by insisting that the church must be more engaged in society and social change. Thus, while action training attempted to engage in a contextual form of theological education, the context in terms of the church's vitality shifted, resulting in a movement that was not in touch with the rising indigenous churches. It may also be that, in some sense, as action training became part of the academic landscape, it was increasingly co-opted by the very system it sought to reform.

The Emergence of Theological Education by Extension:
An Alternative Model from the Developing World

Begun in 1963 by the Evangelical Presbyterian Seminary of Guatemala, theological education by extension (TEE) was an attempt to meet the needs of a rapidly expanding church. TEE was developed through the efforts of missionaries who lived and ministered at the level of the people with whom they worked. The established seminary seemed able to prepare people for ministry only in the few city churches as opposed to

14. Sect is used here in its sociological understanding. See Ernst Troeltsch, *The Social Teachings of the Christian Church,* 2 vols., trans. Olive Wyon, introduction by H. Richard Niebuhr (New York: Macmillan, 1931; reprint, New York: Harper & Row, 1961; originally published in German in 1911); Max Weber, *The Sociology of Religion,* trans. Ephraim Fischoff (Boston: Beacon Press, 1922; reprint, 1963); and H. Richard Niebuhr, *The Social Sources of Denominationalism* (New York: Holt, Rinehart, and Winston, Inc., 1929; reprint, Gloucester, Mass.: Peter Smith, 1987), for a discussion of church-sect typology. See also Milton Yinger, *The Scientific Study of Religion* (New York: Macmillan, 1970).

equipping those in the burgeoning number of rural and village congregations, where much of the ministry was carried on by the laity. Most of the pastors of these rural congregations received their training while "on the job," working alongside the missionaries. Their training did not consist of term papers and the like in a residential setting. TEE's fundamental distinction was between training leaders already engaged in active ministry (the present) and training younger leaders who felt "called" to be leaders in the future (in-service versus pre-service training). The genius of theological education by extension — taking the seminary to the people in their own life context and setting — contributed to its rapid spread. TEE's roots were rural, but it was quickly adapted to the urban context and is found in some form in most major cities, particularly in Latin America.

TEE challenged the established understanding of residential seminaries, the professional paradigm, and how one should do theological education. In this manner it was similar to action training in its critique of the residential seminary program and the status quo of theological education. Men like Ralph Winter, James Emery, and F. Ross Kinsler quickly realized that residential seminary training did not begin to provide the needed leadership for a church that was rapidly growing. An alternative to the residential pattern of theological education was needed. Ralph Winter stated the problem this way:

> Few church movements in the world today operate in such a way as to assimilate to pastoral leadership those members among them most gifted for such ministry. Rather, the churches of the world, especially in the Western world where roots are deep, and where the example to the rest of the world is unfortunately influential, have almost all tended to go over to a professional system that makes pastoral ministry a profession you train for, like medicine or law, rather than a leadership role like that of a mayor or a senator, for which you are elected.[15]

In other words, Winter's critique lent support to an approach that emphasized indigenous development of church leaders from within each congregation.

15. Ralph D. Winter, "Preface," in *The Extension Movement in Theological Education*, p. x.

Theological education by extension could be defined in many different ways. Winter's definition is perhaps as good as any: "That form of education which yields to the life cycle of the student, does not destroy or prevent his [sic] productive relation to society, and does not make the student fit into the needs of a 'residential' school."[16] By accepting this definition, TEE showed clearly that it was not simply another teaching methodology. It was an alternative method of selection. Put another way, TEE's purpose was to equip and empower for ministry those best suited for it, while already engaged in ministry.

Kinsler asks six questions that advocate change in theological education. They are important questions to note, for they cut to the heart of the matter in defining the purposes of theological education, by extension or traditional. Each of the questions Kinsler raises is discussed below:

What is the ministry? Kinsler notes that the entire church should be involved in ministry, and that the primary roles of church leaders should be to equip and empower the congregation for ministry (Eph. 4:11-16). Leadership should arise within the natural context of the church.

Can the people participate fully in theological study and ministry? In his affirmative answer, Kinsler cites examples from church history: John Wesley's class structure, the expansion of the Methodist and Baptist churches on the western frontier of the United States, and the Pentecostal church in Latin America.

Who are the leaders? Sociologically this question encompasses the definition of leadership, the formation of leaders, and their eventual selection and investiture of authority. The Western pattern of conferring ministerial leadership to younger students who are pulled out of their social context, given educational credentials, and then placed back into the churches, unproven, flew in the face of biblical, historical, and theological teaching. Kinsler notes that the "question here raised is not the level of training; a high level of training can be arranged in several different ways. But the ministry is not fundamentally a profession; it is a function in the body of believers."

How can the leaders be trained? This question is an educational one, touching on structure, methods, and educational philosophy. The tra-

16. Winter, "Preface," p. ix.

ditional pattern of theological education requires moving up a pyramid of educational experiences from primary schooling to the seminary as a graduate institution, guaranteeing fewer and fewer people being trained as one approaches the pyramid's apex. The clergy/laity distinction is reinforced. Kinsler sees that real education is not merely acquiring information but doing something with it. The question, What is the meaning of the information as it relates to life? becomes the organizing force. Information is seen less as something to accumulate and more as something to be utilized.

What kind of theological education can we afford? As students move up the educational pyramid, costs increase, affecting not only the students but also the churches, who then must pay salaries appropriate to a professional position. In addition, the maintenance of seminary programs is costly in itself.

What are the goals of our theological training programs? Theological education is not to be a goal itself but exists to serve the church. Every congregation can use existing resources to fulfill the goal of having adequate pastoral leadership. Second, theological education cannot be limited simply to training pastoral leadership; it must engage the entire congregation in wrestling with the issues of modern society.[17]

While the structures and designs of TEE programs vary in specific details, their basic operational premise has been encapsulated in the now famous "split-rail fence" analogy, first popularized by Ted Ward of Michigan State University. Self-study or cognitive input is combined with the person's field experience (ministry). A programmed textbook or material designed for at-home study may be one vehicle to provide the cognitive input (theory). As students go about their ministry, they may discover questions about how their cognitive learning and their experience interrelate. Seminars are offered to provide opportunities to reflect upon the cognitive input and upon experiences in the field. The aim of the seminars is to provide opportunities for the learner to integrate theoretical material with practical experience. An action/reflection model of learning — praxis — is utilized. The seminars can vary in their frequency and approach, being easily adapted to fit the needs of

---

17. F. Ross Kinsler, *The Extension Movement in Theological Education: A Call to the Renewal of the Ministry,* rev. ed. (Pasadena, Calif.: William Carey Library, 1981), pp. 8-24.

the individual participants. The specific methods used in the seminars can also vary depending upon the technologies available.

To some extent all of the case studies presented in this book wrestle with the six questions posed by theological education by extension. A student coming to the Center for Urban Theological Studies (CUTS) or to the Center for Urban Ministerial Education (CUME) will discover that classes are held in the evening to accommodate working people. Thus, one is able to take a course that is affordable, accessible, and immediately applicable to the ministry setting. Both laity and clergy can participate without the dislocation of pulling up roots and moving into a residential theological program.

Consider the case of Maria Rivera. As a deacon in her United Methodist Church, Maria was attracted to CUME because of a class on evangelism. She wanted to take the course to become a better deacon, citing the fact that she hadn't been in school for many years. Already a successful entrepreneur with several multi-level marketing companies, Maria was clearly a gifted communicator. Her initial course experience was positive. Because of the course location and schedule, she returned to take additional courses, eventually completing her ten-course diploma and then the Master of Religious Education degree. Throughout her time of study, she took on increasing responsibilities in her denomination and eventually was called to pastor a small Hispanic congregation. Maria completed her M.Div. and D.Min. degrees while actively pastoring three separate congregations in two states. Without the resources of the seminary coming to her community, contextualized to her reality, she would not have been able to achieve these ministry aspirations.

Location and time schedules are only a part of the struggle for contextualization. Programs like CUTS and CUME have had to wrestle with the overall goal of theological education and its extension to the entire church, affecting methodology, administrative policies, and organizational structures. The influence of theological education by extension on both CUTS and CUME is direct. Perhaps, TEE's greatest impact may be seen in its potential to question how and to whom theological education is delivered, particularly when ethnic constituencies in our cities are considered.

Not Just Seminaries:
The Importance of Bible Institutes

While action training and theological education by extension offered critiques of seminary education as it was practiced in the 1950 and 1960s, a third movement for urban church leadership training cannot be ignored, even though it fell outside of the seminaries. Bible institutes have played and continue to play a prominent role in urban areas. For many people, the local Bible institute serves a discipleship function as well as being a practical training ground for ministerial development and practice.

Bible institutes began in the 1870s in the United States and England. Dwight L. Moody and A. B. Simpson are identified as being at the heart of the American Bible Institute movement.[18] Common themes that emerge from the founding of Bible institutes and continue to guide many of them in their varied forms are: "a concern for the city, a vision to equip lay persons, and a commitment to practical application of training. The institutes were not established to compete with seminaries, but to complement their work, by equipping people within congregations to fill in the gaps the clergy were unable to fill because of limited time and limited individual capacity."[19]

Bible institutes come in many forms. Some were developed by denominations or local congregations to provide for intentional study of the Bible, practical ministry, and theology, typically through the doctrinal filter of the sponsoring denomination or church. Other institutes were developed by denominational judicatories to prepare candidates for ordination credentials. Still other institutes, developed by a particular congregation with a particular denominational or theological bias, are open to Christians from other churches. Finally, there are

18. Jonathan N. Thigpen, "A Brief History of the Bible Institute Movement in America," *Journal of Adult Training* 1 (1994): 1. For a case study of two Hispanic Bible institutes in Massachusetts, see Elizabeth Conde-Frazier, "A Case Study of Two Hispanic Bible Institutes in Massachusetts: Their Mission, Educational Philosophy and Pedagogy" (Ph.D. diss., Boston College, 1998).

19. Kim Davidson, "Demystifying Bible Institutes," in *Educating Urban Christians in the 21st Century: A Needs Assessment for Boston* (Boston: Emmanuel Gospel Center for the Boston Education Collaborative, 1998), p. 116.

those institutes that were developed as independent programs with no specific ties to a particular congregation or denomination.[20]

Kim Davidson, former Project Director for the Boston Education Collaborative, writes: "when contrasted to Bible colleges and Christian liberal arts colleges, Bible institutes immediately manifest some distinguishing characteristics, such as open enrollment policies, and the flexibility to contextualize curriculum to specific various linguistic, ethnic, and cultural communities."[21] Students attracted to Bible institutes tend to be active members of their local congregation, older in age, and established in their community/family/life setting. They come to the institute's program wishing to prepare for some form of lay ministry or to explore their own ministerial calling. Open enrollment, low tuition costs, and flexible schedules and curriculum are additional hallmarks of such programs. For many students, their success at a local Bible institute is the first time they receive positive validation for their educational endeavors. Many are so motivated that they continue their studies at higher levels.

In many urban ethnic church communities, the Bible institute has been, and to a large extent continues to be, the primary educational vehicle for ministerial preparation. Independent churches continue to practice an apprenticeship model of ministerial training and formation, much like that of earlier days. One is not granted ministerial standing based upon educational prerequisites being fulfilled via attendance at a seminary or divinity school, but rather on charismatic and spirit-directed pastoral practice. Thus, there is a fluidity of leadership that follows demonstrated success in ministry. Someone can rise rapidly through the various levels of church leadership without necessarily obtaining "proper" credentials. Bible institutes have served as the initial, and in many cases the only, formal training of leaders in Hispanic and Black churches.

Azusa Pacific University's Haggard School of Theology recognizes the place that Bible institutes play in the Hispanic community and partners with "institutos" to build upon the experience and education graduates have gained. CUTS and CUME have both informal and formal relationships with Bible institutes in order to strengthen and en-

20. Davidson, "Demystifying Bible Institutes," pp. 113-14.
21. Davidson, "Demystifying Bible Institutes," p. 114.

courage rather than compete with their programs. CUTS has agreements with several established Bible institutes and grants advanced standing to students who complete the institutes' full program. Thelma was such a person. She completed a three-year Bible institute diploma and was able to enroll in a degree program that built upon the foundation she received through the institute.

The role of Bible institutes in understanding the dynamics of urban theological education as they relate to the changing social and historical contexts of our cities must not be overlooked. At the same time that many larger, established, old-line churches were experiencing rapid membership losses in their urban congregations, the vitality of the church was quietly shifting to independent, Pentecostal, Charismatic, and Evangelical churches as well as to newer, ethnic churches of the mainline denominations. Much of this shift can be attributed to the continuing ethnic transitions in our cities. The Bible institutes serve an important role in the delivery of urban theological education to these independent and ethnic congregations. Many attendees and graduates, because they lack the requisite educational credentials to attend seminary, were denied access to higher education. This is not to suggest that the Bible institutes provide inferior education. On the contrary, it is rather a harsh indictment against the seminaries for failing to recognize that their model of leadership preparation missed the very lifeblood of the city — those already engaged in ministry. In a very real sense, the complaint that the seminaries and universities were "out of touch" with the city was justifiable. Bluntly put, they were.

Community Involvement: The Public Ministry Challenge

Lawrence Cremin has termed the period from 1876 to 1980 as the "Metropolitan Period." This was a time when education, among other things, was increasingly popularized and made more accessible. During this period, Protestantism in the United States experienced profound change as it responded to modernity and the challenges initiated by the industrial revolution and the rise of capitalism along with its class inequalities.[22]

22. Lawrence Cremin, *American Education: The Metropolitan Experience 1876-1980* (New York: Harper and Row, 1988), p. 19.

Two distinct Christian viewpoints emerged in the urbanizing culture. The first favored an ethical Christianity directed to everyday life (the so-called "social gospel"), which emphasized social transformation. The second view was the fundamentalist response, which saw the world as increasingly evil. One's only hope was to be saved from the world, hence an emphasis on individual conversion (evangelism).

In no small measure, the Bible institutes arose from the fundamentalist impulse.[23] In the late 1940s the emergence of the neofundamentalists, the "Evangelicals," is an important historical development. This movement attempted to retain the fundamentals of the faith while at the same time becoming more engaged in social concerns. Overlaying this dynamic was the emergence of the Pentecostal movement. In the city one finds churches from each of these historic movements as well as variations on each theme. However, whether one embraced the importance of transforming deplorable social conditions or chose to ignore the social to emphasize the individual, the fact is that urban churches have had to wrestle with the role of the church in larger society. The "public ministry" of the church is only the latest label for the age-old tension. An interesting aspect of the public dimension of ministry can be seen in the rise of community organizing. Modern community organizing originated in the 1930s in Chicago, under Saul Alinsky, founder of the Industrial Areas Foundation. Sato and Miller write:

> Alinsky succeeded in coalescing the ethnic parishes of the Catholic Church community, organized labor, voluntary associations, and neighborhood residents into a single organization called Back of the Yards Neighborhood Council. The process of organizing these disparate groups into a unified force became the basis for modern community organizing, and, over time, churches, synagogues, and other religious institutions became focal points for community organizers and their national and regional networks. As the labor

23. Various textbooks on church history provide additional details regarding the modernist/fundamentalist split in American Protestantism. See Mark A. Noll, *A History of Christianity in the United States and Canada* (Grand Rapids: Eerdmans, 1992), or Bruce L. Shelly, *Church History in Plain Language,* updated 2nd edition, with a foreword by Mark Noll (Dallas: Word Publishing, 1995).

movement's interest in a broad social and economic justice agenda waned, Alinsky's focus shifted to the religious community.[24]

For decades, much of community organizing has involved segments of the Catholic Church and mainline Protestant churches. The more theologically "conservative" church communities have not participated in community organizing to a great degree, with the exception of some African-American churches. While the Evangelical, Pentecostal, and Holiness churches are among the fastest-growing churches in the United States, they have been conspicuously absent from community organizing. However, this is slowly changing.[25] Seminaries and other institutions of higher education have begun to include community organizing and development as part of their curricula. This is an encouraging sign.

The case study, "A Metro Strategy," highlights some of the struggles that a particular parish faces when it begins to consider its public ministry role. Profound questions arise about the nature and meaning of the ministry. For Father John such questions cut at the heart of the church's mission — who or what is to be transformed by the gospel — individuals, structures, or both? The decision to participate in a community-organizing effort is rightly recognized as reframing one's orientation and understanding of the church's ministry.

Summary: Reframing Is Necessary

This brief historical survey has set the broad context that gave rise to the six urban theological education programs introduced in the following case studies and to others not covered in this work. Founders and developers of the six programs attempted to be more contextualized to

24. Timothy Sato and Donald E. Miller, "Christians Supporting Community Organizing: A New Voice for Change among Evangelical, Holiness and Pentecostal Christians," Center for Religion and Civic Culture, University of Southern California, 1999, p. 2.

25. For instance, Christians Supporting Community Organizing is a national effort to encourage Evangelical, Holiness, and Pentecostal churches to become involved in community-organizing efforts in their local areas. For more information, contact CSCO at P.O. Box 8766, Denver, CO 80201.

their reality. The programs represent a holy dissatisfaction with the status quo of theological education as the developers discerned it. Seminaries and Bible institutes both have been, and continue to be, dominated by the schooling paradigm.

Inherent in these six programs is the assumption that ministry transcends the role of clergy. Lay involvement and mobilization of the entire church for ministry, both inside the church and in larger society, are themes that guided their formation and development. The case study on New York Theological Seminary (NYTS) clearly demonstrates this. By offering theological education within the walls of a prison, NYTS attempts to respond to the particular needs of a particular constituency — prisoners, who are unable to participate in traditional theological education programs. Issues of empowering the powerless are quite profound as you will notice in studying this particular case. In some ways, all six programs, whether connected to theological institutions or apart from them, critique the traditional way of teaching theology, implying that it is too restricted to an elite group of persons, and all attempt to deal with the concept of lay involvement, each offering its own unique perspective.

Most of the programs outlined in this book continue to wrestle with the challenge of when to prepare people for ministry. Traditionally and historically, many churches and denominations have moved to the pre-service model of theological education. While this is useful and has educational merits, most of the models highlighted here attempt to modify this approach. Several have chosen to organize themselves around an "in-service" model of education, that is, to provide educational content for persons already engaged in ministry, not just training for ministry in the future. Elements of praxis — ministerial practice and reflection — are important themes that emerge from the history of the six cases. All of the models have had to wrestle with the questions of how theological education is delivered, to whom it is delivered, by whom, and for what purpose.

Community is another theme that emerges from our historical survey. In most of the cases presented, issues of empowerment, development, and organization are present in some form. For some, like "Metro Strategy," this is the raison d'être; for others it is more implicit. However, all of the programs recognize the crucial importance of engaging the community for transformation. All continue to wrestle with the appropriate role of the church in service to the community. Obviously a continuum is established here, but community is a key theme that has emerged in all six of the programs. For the more evangelical programs, this means emphasizing more strongly the social aspects of the gospel. For programs with a more mainline bent, issues of urban spirituality to match social witness emerge as cutting edges. Both are expressions of a concern to involve and engage the church in the wider affairs of the community — a public ministry, if you will. Evident in every one of the six cases is the element of providing tools for students to engage in critical reflection about the nature of the church and its involvement in the community. Skills such as social analysis, ethical reflection, and biblical/theological exegesis are important tools that are taught via a variety of pedagogical approaches. Most importantly, students are encouraged to learn how to reflect critically on their ministry in light of the ever-changing urban environment.

At the juncture of the twenty-first century, these six programs represent concrete responses to specific historical, social, and educational contexts. They are critiques of continuing to do "business as usual." All of them have sought, to varying degrees, to mediate the observed tension between traditional theological education and the ever-changing dynamics of the city. Observing their struggles as well as their success should provide us with fodder to work at reframing theological education for urban ministry. The authors invite you to join us in this journey.

Using Case Studies in
Urban Theological Education

ALICE FRAZER EVANS AND ROBERT A. EVANS

"Liberating education consists in acts of cognition, not transference of information."[1]

PAOLO FREIRE

The group of twenty urban educators gathered in Puerto Rico from across the United States. The meeting began with an energetic discussion of the case study, "A Metro Strategy." Their dialogue moved to penetrating discussion of the mission of the church and insightful analysis of a bold, parish-based initiative to train clergy and lay leaders for urban ministry. This focused discussion shaped the tone for the next two days of meetings by enhancing the quality of discourse and by enabling those gathered to hear and appreciate the different perspectives at the table.

The authors developed the six case studies in the following chapters for clergy and lay church leaders committed to transformative and transforming ministry in cities. Cases are especially helpful in stimulating reflection and dialogue among students, faculty, administrators, and trustees at centers for theological education. These cases also hold

---

1. Paolo Freire, *Pedagogy of the Oppressed* (New York: Herder and Herder, 1972), p. 67.

the potential for informing and enabling discussion among denominational leaders from different theological perspectives. Those funding education for urban ministry should also be involved since the cases explore a variety of paradigms for urban ministry. Our intent is to use the cases as lively vehicles to draw this growing and vibrant constituency into serious and creative conversations about the most effective and faithful ways to reframe education for urban ministry.

There are many types of case studies, ranging from hypothetical situations and one-page "verbatims" to book-length, historical accounts of complex situations. The case studies in this volume, such as "A Metro Strategy," follow the style of case used by the Association for Case Teaching and Harvard Business School. These concise cases tell the story of an actual, unresolved, problematic situation at a particular point in time. The context and events of each case are seen through the eyes of one person who is challenged to make a decision. Since the six cases describe events at only one moment in the life of ever-changing institutions, names of the primary players are disguised. This approach protects the privacy of those persons involved and helps provide critical distance for the reader from present events, programs, and personnel at these institutions. Persons reading and discussing the case are invited to "enter" the situation, identify the primary issues and players in the case, analyze the problems, and work together to discuss — or debate — the most appropriate responses to the case problems and defend the rationale for their proposals.

Brazilian educator Paolo Freire highlights the value of the problem-posing dimension of this particular type of case study. Freire's sharp critique of "banking education" contrasts with his advocacy for problem-posing education in which a community learns together.[2] Rather than "depositing" predetermined information into the student, a case leader has the opportunity to become a co-learner. The community of learners listens to one another, challenges their own and one another's perceptions, and builds on one another's insights to resolve the case problems. These are essential ingredients of liberating education that frees learners from preconceived resolutions to minister creatively and cooperatively in the ever-changing context of the city.

Elliot Eisner writes that much of current educational theory and

2. Freire, *Pedagogy of the Oppressed,* pp. 57-64.

practice is dominated by a scientific approach that gives students little room to participate in the creation of their own educational programming. A teacher's emphasis is usually on predictability, control, rational outcomes, or measurable objectives. Consequently, educators divide the curriculum into ever-smaller pieces of information and tasks, rendering a view of the whole almost impossible and seriously limiting student curiosity and legitimate inquiry.[3]

Using problem-posing case studies has the potential to counter this pattern as well as meet some of the distinctive needs of urban theological education. A well-written, problem-posing case describes not only a dilemma but the persons involved and their context, including the setting and historical background. The details of each case are considered in relationship to the whole. A discussion of individuals, alternatives, and principles rests on the factual information as well as the context. In addition, while each case has clear themes, the outcome of a case discussion is unknown prior to the actual teaching event, allowing for spontaneity and freedom of inquiry. The dialogical nature of a case discussion encourages participants to draw on their own experiences and heightens the possibility of learning from one another. These are particularly appropriate attributes of case discussions in an urban, multicultural setting to which theological students bring rich and varied life experiences.

Cases also draw on the power of storytelling, which is at the heart of communicating social and moral precepts in many of the cultures that meet in contemporary urban centers. People are drawn into stories, a fact evidenced by Jesus in the Master Teacher's use of parables. Not unlike the people involved in case discussions, Jesus told good stories — and asked challenging questions. Narrative, as opposed to linear, propositional presentation, gives learners freedom to interact and dialogue with the story. They are able to identify life issues with the characters in the mini-drama before them and draw implications from the case. The open-ended nature of the case allows the participants to utilize their own experiences and reflections not only to personalize the case, but to address issues that confront them in their own ministry. In looking at a case that relates to our own challenges, we frequently glean

---

3. Elliot W. Eisner, *The Educational Imagination: On the Design and Evaluation of School Programs* (New York: Macmillan, 1985), pp. 17-20.

ideas that a rational, linear approach may overlook. For example, if a school principal is dealing with a student who is consistently absent from school, the typical answer is punishment, often by suspending the student from school. This punishment obviously results in absence from school — the very problem that needs to be addressed! Urban ministry programs confronted by growing student needs and shifting institutional budgets are seldom saved by slashing programs and staff.

Isolation of persons and groups is normative in urban settings where populations are often transient and divided by race, class, and culture. The participatory and dialogical nature of a well-facilitated case discussion can lead participants to identify others in the discussion with similar needs and concerns. Their exchange provides a non-threatening opportunity to begin to build relationships with other city dwellers and learn to trust others' biblically and theologically informed insights on the problems under discussion. Honest dialogue about shared concerns from a faith perspective is a foundational step toward building community — a promise of the gospel which is difficult, but possible, to realize.

While case teaching can liberate a classroom for new levels of learning, there are risks involved. In the hands of an instructor used to offering cold facts, the case can be little more than a façade for depositing preconceived notions into the learners' minds. Rather than empowering participants to ask their real questions and be open to different perspectives, a case leader who announces an "open" discussion and proceeds to supply "the answers" effectively shuts down future opportunities for genuine dialogue. An effective case leader must be skilled in the art of teaching, calling forth various ways of knowing and learning, and contextualizing the case discussion to the specific group. Case teaching calls for knowing the case as well as the learning group and tailoring the approach to encourage dialogue, creativity, and application to life.

We have designed the text to support teaching that encourages "acts of cognition — not transference of information." Each case is accompanied by a set of teaching notes with suggested discussion questions and approaches for case facilitators. Rather than viewing these notes as models or predetermined lesson plans, we see them as supplements to facilitators' own creative designs for gaining the maximum benefit from each case and set of commentaries. The contrasting commentaries that follow each case are also intended to stimulate dialogue and deepen insights into the practical, theoretical, and theological issues raised by the cases. We encourage both individual readers and discussion groups to be in dialogue with the case commentators who draw on their own rich experiences to offer their perspectives on a specific case. For the greatest educational benefit, we urge facilitators of group discussions to allow participants sufficient advance notice and suggested guidelines for studying the case well before a plenary discussion. Advance small group discussions guided by a set of questions are also a helpful way to "prime the pump" for deeper insights in the plenary session.

Recording the essence of discussion contributions in an ordered sequence is an effective way not only to monitor speakers, show the progression of the discussion, and point out connections between points, but also to develop a record of the discussion that is particularly beneficial to visual learners. For these reasons, we urge facilitators to consider in advance the organization of the board or newsprint on which the developing case discussion is traced and then record the core of each person's contributions in illuminating categories. The incorporation of audiovisual aids, culturally appropriate exercises, and "minilectures" as the need arises, all enhance the possibility for challenging and liberating learning with cases. The case leader's knowledge and insights are important — often crucial, but the timing and style of sharing these determine whether a community learns together or the leader's contributions essentially "kill" a vibrant learning experience.

We alert case facilitators to an additional concern about using case studies as an educational tool in group discussions, particularly in multicultural settings. Without careful monitoring, case discussions tend to favor more verbal participants, putting at a disadvantage those who are not using their first language, who may be shy, or who have been acculturated to be reserved or even submissive in a classroom setting. The entire group can be deprived of their insights, and those who feel ignored may withdraw in frustration. Eric Law, an Episcopal priest experienced in multicultural facilitation, notes a more subtle form of discrimination.[4] He refers to studies which show that in multicultural

---

4. Eric Law, *The Wolf Shall Dwell with the Lamb: A Spirituality for Leadership in Multicultural Community* (St. Louis: Chalice Press, 1993).

settings white men and women of Northern European descent speak more assertively and, often unconsciously, dominate discussions. A potentially destructive dynamic can be countered by moving to small group discussions with appointed leaders or balancing contributions by being culturally sensitive to quiet signals from those who wish to speak.

These six experience-based, problem-posing cases are designed to contextualize critical issues facing theological education. We hope that the case studies will invite readers to join us in the challenge of reframing education for urban ministry. We also trust that these examples of education for urban ministry will provoke creative, communal, and culturally relevant responses that lead to revitalization of the practice of urban ministry.

Case studies have the potential to nurture wisdom. Real wisdom involves the integration of theory and practice or of discernment and application. Urban practitioners live at the heart of the traumatic and transforming issues of contemporary culture. Their confessional, pragmatic, and inspirational "city savvy," however, occasionally needs to be nurtured toward "urban wisdom." Learning in community, sharing one's faith and life experiences, risking new ideas, and being open to the Spirit as it speaks to us through one another are all elements that lead to wisdom and transformed ministry to the city.

II. CASE STUDIES AND COMMENTARIES ON CRITICAL ISSUES FACING URBAN THEOLOGICAL EDUCATION

Case Study: Another World

Carlos Moran, the Associate Dean for Urban and Multi-Cultural Studies at Azusa Pacific University, wondered who was calling him at home on a Tuesday night at 10:30 P.M. "Dean, sorry to bother you at home. This is Professor Charles Armand. I just returned from teaching my first class in our new Urban Center in South Central L.A. I need to see you in the morning to discuss this teaching assignment. It's another world working with these African-American, Hispanic and Korean students, and I'm not sure I'm prepared to continue."

"Dr. Armand, I would be pleased to meet with you first thing in the morning to talk about your concerns. Remember that several of your faculty colleagues have found teaching on our urban campus to be challenging, but also very rewarding."

As Carlos hung up the phone, he realized how committed he was to having the university's School of Theology deliver on providing urban theological education in the heart of Los Angeles. He believed that the gospel message to "love your neighbor as yourself" called Christians to enter the world of other children of God who have different cultural and ethnic traditions. Carlos recalled some of his words of introduction to the Urban Center program in an address to the faculty: "We are invited to see how the threads of our existence intertwine.

This case was written by Robert A. Evans and Alice Frazer Evans. Copyright © The Case Study Institute. The names of all persons in this case are disguised to protect the privacy of the individuals involved.

These encounters make my understanding of the world richer. An immersion in another culture enables me to return to my own cultural tradition with a more diverse, colorful, and meaningful understanding of the mosaic."

Carlos's vision for the School of Theology faculty members was that they could recontextualize their understanding of the gospel by encountering a new constituency on their own turf in South Central Los Angeles. For some faculty members, this was already bringing a kind of conversion to their understanding of urban theological education. The issue was how to help faculty members like Charles Armand catch the vision and share its fruits for themselves as well as for their students on both campuses.

The motivation for the urban program and establishment of the Urban Center had its roots in a response to the 1992 Los Angeles uprising and in the vision of a new university president. The events of the early 1990s introduced a new consciousness of greater Los Angeles as an extremely diverse, multiethnic, and multi-economic reality. The president, appointed in 1990, brought energy and vision to what he hoped would be a renewal of Christian commitment to revitalize the wider community of Christian scholars and disciples. Like the university, many of the school's sponsoring churches were located in suburban areas outside the city center. These churches also expressed a renewed call to be engaged with the city. With the support of their congregations, university strategic planning teams began to design new programs and designate scholarship monies for African-American and Hispanic students.

One of the planning goals was to create a new kind of college to respond to the most urgent issues and problems of North American urban centers. Rather than a place where "professors get tenure and students get credentials," this was to be an institution focused on the public good. To implement the vision, the university hired Carlos Moran as Associate Dean for Urban and Multi-Cultural Studies. He had direct access to the president and the provost to mobilize the program.

The Urban Center was opened in 1995 in alliance with the World Impact Center, a long-standing community ally located in South Central Los Angeles. The School of Theology would introduce and staff the first set of courses on the new urban campus, with the anticipation that other university schools would follow.

The Urban Center sought to recognize that racial and ethnic issues in Los Angeles were no longer primarily "black and white." Thirty-five percent of southern California and 54 percent of South Central Los Angeles residents were now Latinos, several hundred thousand of whom were illegal immigrants. At the same time, the state was in a slowly recovering economy. One of the School of Theology's goals was to help urban congregations face these new realities at a particularly perilous time.

Carlos was convinced that public reaction to the demographic and economic shifts had led to the recent introduction of state propositions to restrict or eliminate illegal immigrant access to tax-supported social benefits, remove affirmative-action hiring policies, and eliminate "set-asides" for ethnic and minority groups. He believed the church needed to develop more responsible alternatives and new leadership models to address this reaction. The Urban Center also needed faculty members who understood the political and social issues and were able to equip and empower students who often had inadequate theological training and very little experience dealing with political systems. Faculty from the School of Theology worked with the School of Business to develop a Bachelor of Science degree in Christian leadership to accomplish some of these goals.

In order to address the fact that many students' first language was not English, Carlos introduced courses with bilingual components in Spanish and Korean. Limited English-proficient students (LEPS) studied their first twenty units in their native language. The second twenty units were bilingual English and Spanish or Korean. LEPS students received a lecture of forty-five minutes to an hour and then broke to "debrief" the lecture with a Spanish- or Korean-speaking tutor by discussing the material and asking questions. LEPS students were required to take the final twenty units toward their degree in English.

Carlos also realized that the university plan to utilize the present School of Theology faculty meant re-equipping them to teach and relate to a different constituency while delivering a quality and relevant form of education. He decided to present to the Dean the possibility of a summer Spanish course and to encourage all faculty members to enroll.

Charles Armand's telephone call confirmed the significant challenges of developing the Urban Center program with an overwhelmingly Euro-American, male, middle-class faculty who all lived in suburbia. Several minority faculty appointments to teach Urban Center courses had been made at the adjunct level under Carlos's leadership, but the core faculty was basically unchanged. Most if not all of these faculty members were evangelical Christians with a Wesleyan heritage and strong commitments to the school's historic sense of social mission. However, Carlos also knew it was extremely difficult for the majority of those with a discipline-oriented, guild-dominated, classical theological education to shift their style of teaching. His colleagues in the program were going through a re-education, if not a conversion process, of their own.

Carlos acknowledged that his bicultural upbringing in New Mexico with an immigrant Mexican father and a mother from a traditional Spanish-American family gave him a distinct advantage. The world in which he grew up taught him to share the world of those different from himself and to learn to integrate those experiences into his own. In contrast, he recalled colleagues who had unloaded on him the anxiety and fear they experienced in some of their visits to the Urban Center.

Early in the program, a frustrated biblical scholar met him in the hallway. "Carlos, I get down to the city and there's nowhere to park. With the number of car thefts in the area, I bought one of those clubs to put on my steering wheel. I never know if my car will be there when I get out of class, and as I walk to class, I wonder whether I'll be mugged coming or going. It's very difficult to teach effectively with this kind of anxiety." Carlos remembered asking his colleague whether the biblical account was not populated by ordinary people, disciples, and even prophets who experienced levels of anxiety and fear. Since the scholar's students were as vulnerable as the faculty in these areas of the city, Carlos hoped he might recognize a common ground of vulnerability that would help him better understand and communicate an incarnate gospel of death and resurrection.

Another colleague in theology explained how students tried to negotiate his course reading assignments. To Carlos the colleague seemed both offended and fascinated by the different cultural approaches. "A few weeks into the course, a group of Korean students invited me to a meal after class. During dinner, they proceeded to negotiate the assignments from ten books to six. In the end, we compromised at eight. Their world appeared to revolve around negotiating about everything, and it was their expectation that they could do this in terms of reading assignments as well." The professor continued by expressing that Hispanic students often had a different way of approaching the questions of scholarly obligation. They would not publicly object to what he knew were heavy reading demands for those already engaged in full-time activities. Rather than objecting or re-negotiating, they simply did a basic amount of the reading and did not engage in public discussion of what they had no intention of pursuing. Perhaps his experience represented two different styles of negotiating life. Carlos reminded the colleague that his Anglo students on the main campus also negotiated assignments. They just took a different approach.

Carlos arranged for Urban Center faculty to make reports at School of Theology faculty retreats and some regular faculty meetings. His goal was to promote greater understanding of the urban program and to encourage other faculty to take on assignments. Eventually every course had the required faculty.

Carlos recalled the great appreciation one professor expressed for the generosity of his students at community events that were organized in conjunction with the class. "I was very moved by both the time and money that students invested in preparing special dishes for their classmates. There was a degree of generosity and biblical hospitality that I have never experienced on our safe, suburban campus."

"The level of students' understanding and their ability to share how the Bible has shaped and informed their lives offer an amazing witness." A professor of church history made this affirmation and then declared, "My students at the Urban Center have a lived experience with church history out of their congregations and out of their understanding of tradition. The Euro-American students in my main campus classes draw on a richer academic background in history, but they don't seem as responsive to the way in which God intervenes in history, especially with His people."

Another faculty member noted, "My students have been so appreciative of my presence in the Urban Center. Before the center opened, most inner city students with families and jobs had enormous difficulty with the long commute to the main campus for courses. They also express gratitude for the opportunity to increase their knowledge and their skills of ministry to serve their people. These opportunities are taken for granted by my other students."

As Carlos reached to turn off the light by the telephone, he glanced at his notes from recent conversations with students in the Urban Center about their educational experience.

John Barnes, a full-time salesman and pastor of an African-American congregation, declared,

> I am amazed that my professors, who have so much formal education, have so little knowledge of the conditions under which we live with our families and serve our people. They interpret a car backfiring as a gunshot. They don't have any comprehension of the very real threats my family, my parishioners, and I negotiate every day on streets that are increasingly violent and drug-infested. They don't understand the restrictions we face all the time in keeping our congregations whole in the midst of poverty and corrupt politicians. Things are just not as neatly packaged out here.
>
> I am also hurt by the blindness of the university bureaucracy about registration, grades, and scholarship. Carlos, we know you are trying to make changes, but the fact that we still have to drive in horrendous traffic for nearly an hour to the main campus to register for classes and to have access to the library is extremely time consuming and difficult for most urban students. Most of us don't have cars, and there is virtually no public transportation between South Central and Azusa.

One of the older Hispanic pastors shared with Carlos his concern about language: "When I have difficulty finding the right English word to express my Latino theology, I wonder if the faculty have forgotten that neither Karl Barth nor Aquinas had English as their mother tongue. I appreciate their effort to come to the Urban Center, but I suspect they don't want to enter my world very deeply. Therefore, it is difficult for them to help me gain the leadership skills I need to serve my people and my city."

Peter Park, who had great respect for the authority of the teacher, asserted, "Faculty seem to value the number of pages I read more than my experiences in ministry that inform the way I read the Bible and the way I see theology. I wish I could help them understand the vitality of the faith in Korea and the tremendous growth of our churches that are in stark contrast to many primarily white suburban congregations. It would also be very helpful if some courses were offered in the evening and on weekends when more people are free to attend class."

Juanita Rodriguez, who was a grassroots organizer in her own community, reflected on her needs as a theological student.

> If faculty members are serious about teaching in the city, they need not only conversion, but transformation. Despite the fact that women are the predominant force, not only in the church, but also in many community organizations, there are almost no women on the core faculty. There are a few adjuncts in subsidiary fields, but women who have great potential as both congregational and community leaders need respected role models.
>
> If Azusa Pacific faculty really want to engage the life of the city and the diversity that is Los Angeles, we need faculty who are like us, who understand our world, who help us interpret the gospel to our people and transform our communities. We don't need all the faculty to look like us, but we need more than we currently have if this is going to be a new model for preparing men and women for urban ministry.

Carlos was startled to hear his wife ask whether he was coming to bed since it was already very late. As he closed the door to his study, Carlos reflected on his own call to urban ministry. He had accepted his position at the university because he had found others who shared his vision for transforming the way in which the university related to the city. He had found wise and skilled faculty and administrators of great faith who expressed their commitment to the city. They welcomed into their world those who were different. But Carlos was not sure they could risk entering other worlds to become co-learners.

Carlos knew there were diamonds in South Central L.A.; it was just that the setting was different. He desperately wanted his faculty colleagues to be able to celebrate and relish their experiences in the Urban Center. He hoped they would learn new ways of teaching and learning, and that they would be as much instructed as instructing in what they were doing in the city. His challenge was discerning how to build this kind of relationship between his teaching colleagues and the students in the program.

As much as he was worried about the faculty, Carlos was probably more concerned about the Urban Center students. He knew that many people who lived in the inner city had a string of broken promises from the universities, churches, or others who had promised to be companions on the way to a more faithful and fulfilling life in the inner city. He hoped the Urban Center would not be another "flash in the pan." He knew that students were often willing to play what they called the "faculty game," but experience had taught them not to raise their hopes too high. Carlos was determined to help the university and the School of Theology keep their promises. He believed deeply in the vision of the Urban Center to become a viable program for the seminary and the churches that wanted to serve the city. They needed to show their love, not just while the budget lasted, but by continuing to be present and by changing the form and location of urban theological education. Carlos was struggling with what needed to be done to make the vision a lasting reality.

Background: Another World
Haggard Graduate School of Theology,
Azusa Pacific University

Azusa Pacific University began in 1899 as Huntington Park Training School for Christian Workers. The school became Azusa Bible College in 1946, attained liberal arts status with mergers in the 1960s with Arlington College and Los Angeles Pacific College, and became a university in 1981. The main campus is located in Azusa, California, formerly considered a suburb of Los Angeles and now an increasingly urban area. By 1998 APU's 4,600 university students were enrolled in 30 undergraduate majors and 12 master's degree programs.

By tradition and practice, the curriculum of the university is undergirded by Charles Wesley's emphasis on issues of social justice, human rights, racial equality, peace, and justice. The university has a clear commitment to underrepresented groups, which make up 25 percent of university enrollment and 55 percent of its School of Theology student body. The university also has a strong volunteer community service program that requires undergraduates to give 30 hours of community or outreach service each semester. This is only one component of the strong Christian faith perspective of Azusa Pacific's programs. The university maintains cooperative agreements with six Protestant denominations (Church of the Brethren, Church of God, Free Methodist Church, Missionary Church, Religious Society of Friends, and the Salvation Army).

The C. P. Haggard Graduate School of Theology (HGST) is one of three graduate schools in the university. HGST defines the context for its programs as both suburban and urban. Many of the school's sponsoring churches are suburban, located in affluent areas in Southern California and in suburban areas in other states. The school's stated goals are to:

- Provide a solid core of academic studies within the several theological disciplines;
- Engage students in experiential learning and integrative academic reflection; and

47

- Serve the global mission of the kingdom of God by preparing people for leadership in the church and for ministries within various cultural and ethnic settings.

HGST has an additional goal of making a "seamless connection" between non-accredited Bible colleges and seminary and university programs and offers certificate level training to support this goal. The HGST certificate program averages more than 400 students, two thirds of whom are male, with a majority of African Americans and Hispanics. This program is designed for lay leaders and pastors seeking continuing education. The average certificate student has completed the tenth year of school, the equivalent of a high school sophomore. The certificate program serves to give students confidence and to identify those who may want to continue on a degree track. Some certificate credits are transferable to university undergraduate degrees and/or toward life experience for HGST degree programs. Certificate programs are taught by Haggard faculty and offered throughout the city in various churches and other ministry centers.

The administration and most classes for HGST are located on the main campus in Azusa. The School of Theology initiated a new, second site for its courses by opening the Urban Center located in South Central Los Angeles. This site is part of a larger goal of the university to develop an urban campus as an "incarnational ministry to the urban context with delivery of all resources available through the University." At the time of this case study, other schools in the university were implementing plans to begin services and programs in Central Los Angeles in subsequent academic years. Urban Center students have access both to the LA campus and the main campus in Azusa. They also have full rights to the same administrative, faculty, library, and classroom resources designated for all university students.

Because the goal of the Urban Center is to make HGST degree programs accessible to urban students, the certificate program is not available at this site. At the time of this case study, the main campus had some 300 students enrolled in degree programs, while the Urban Center averaged between 75 and 85 students. About 60 percent of the Urban Center student body were Asian; 30 percent Hispanic, and some 10 percent African American. Less than 1 percent were women. The age of students in these programs ranged from 22 to 61 years.

Discussion Notes: Another World

Teaching Goals on Contextualization and Constituency

- To explore the connections between biblical mandates and theological assumptions, goals, and programs in urban ministry
- To investigate the connection between mission and contextualization
- To explore the challenges of contextualization
- To explore the implications of partnering in urban ministry

Discussion Approach

I. Context

Ask the participants to share their immediate visual images of the main campus site in Azusa. Do the same for the urban site. Describe the settings for both sites. Identify the resources available in each setting.

Identify the partners that the university relies on to sustain the urban site.

> (Urge participants to expand the concepts of "resources" and "partners.")

II. Issues and Questions for Discussion

A. What are the goals for the urban site?

> Drawing on the historical background of the university and the perspectives of the university president and Carlos Moran:

1. What biblical mandates inform these goals?

2. What is the theological basis for establishing the urban campus? (Consider, for example, Wesleyan social conscience, the Reign of God, or calls to respond to those in need.)

3. How do these mandates or principles influence decisions about the context and constituency of the urban campus?

B. Who "owns" the urban site? Consider, among others, the institutions, the partners, and the constituency. What determines "ownership"?

C. In what specific ways has the School of Theology sought to contextualize education for this particular constituency?

What are the greatest challenges of contextualization? In your discussion consider the cost of contextualization (for example, comfort zone, distance, traditional roles of faculty, and teaching styles). Focus and go more deeply into one or two of the dimensions most relevant to discussion participants (for example, worldview or safety issues).

D. Select one or two of the topics in C.

1. What is the role of pastors, urban site students, partners, or faculty to address these challenges?

2. Consider the implications of equipping existing faculty to be effective in the urban context versus hiring adjuncts from the urban constituency. Draw on concrete examples in the case.

3. What are the costs/benefits for the students involved in educating the faculty for a new context?

III. Alternatives

A. What concrete suggestions do you have for Carlos Moran as he tries to meet the needs of faculty as well as the goals of students and the university in the urban site?

B. Broaden the discussion to the context of the participants. How do the promise and perils of contextualization apply to any ministry in a changing context?

C. What resources can be drawn on to enable a constituency to address the contextualization issue (for example, faith or other people)?

Suggestions for Specific Group Discussion

For practitioners such as pastors, theological students, or urban advocates focus on questions I; II.B, C, D 1, 3; and III.

For representatives of seminary faculty, trustees, and funding agencies or church and denominational representatives, focus on questions I; II.A, C, D 2; and III.A, C.

Case Study: Setting the Captives Free

The monotonous clacking of the Metro North train making its way back to New York City usually had a soothing effect on Paul's mind after the noise and confusion of a day at Sing Sing Prison. That was not the case today. His mind raced ahead to the important conversations he must have with his colleagues at New York Theological Seminary (NYTS). All, including the Board of Trustees, had been behind the initiatives he had proposed in the past including offering a degree at Sing Sing. Would they support this new venture?

The possibilities and potential headaches behind the inmates' request that NYTS begin a certificate program were significant. Paul thought back to the early days of the seminary's work at Sing Sing, a maximum- and mid-security New York State prison housing 2,500 male inmates. According to conventional wisdom, it was not the kind of place where a seminary looked to find potential church leaders. But then, Paul knew that NYTS was not a conventional seminary.

Tracing its roots to the early 1900s with the establishment of The Biblical Seminary in Manhattan, the seminary had undergone many transitions through the years. Each transition had been influenced by an impending crisis and a changing context. Paul's work with the school began at one of those crisis moments. During the late 1950s and through the 1960s, the urban context was radically changing, and the Biblical Seminary administrators were engaged in a continual battle for funds, for students, and for competent faculty. In 1960, the trustees decided that a new image would improve the situation and changed the name of the school to New York Theological Seminary. But in 1969 when he was called from twenty years of experience in innovative urban ministry and a tenured teaching position at Union Seminary to be president of NYTS, Paul knew that the survival of the institution would require much more dramatic and controversial kinds of change.

The early years of his fourteen-year tenure as president were marked by difficult and sometimes painful decisions. Three urgent tasks that had to be confronted were curriculum development, recruitment, and finances. Paul remembered both the turmoil and the excitement of that time. In addition to many hours of discussion and meetings to win over the faculty, Paul wrote numerous letters seeking to win support and shore up the finances. In those letters, he always stressed that the effort was not to maintain and develop another small Protestant seminary in New York City but to press forward with educational experimentation and innovation. He had known all along that NYTS had important assets: a superb location in the heart of New York City, an able faculty, and the freedom to experiment with education for ministry in an urban society.

Within five years, the school had achieved a measure of stability. Even in that short time, Paul remembered that there were some successes and also some failures. The failures were often those programs that he and other seminary administrators thought would meet some very important need. Many of their bright ideas did not take off. The programs that did take hold were, for the most part, those that came about when a group of persons came to the staff and laid before them very clear needs and called for academic programs to meet them. The commitment to education at Sing Sing Prison began with just such an encounter.

Paul clearly recalled the day. In the spring of 1981, Jack Franklin, a Methodist pastor who had served for more than fifteen years as a chaplain in the New York State prison system, and a young Christian Reformed Church clergy person, Carl Dirkma, who had been volunteering one day a week in one of the prisons, came to him with an idea that demanded attention. They explained that over 400 long-term prisoners in various state facilities had acquired accredited college degrees through extension programs. Many of them were Christian and Muslim men of strong faith, eager to continue their higher education. The pastors proposed that NYTS consider offering a graduate degree at a correctional facility. Creating a graduate degree for inmates was the most unconventional idea that had been proposed to the seminary in Paul's time. Unconventional as it seemed, Franklin and Dirkma went away from that meeting knowing that the seminary would do its best to be responsive to this challenging new context and its needs.

The population in New York State prisons was largely African American and Hispanic, with over 70 percent of the inmates coming from and returning to New York metro problem areas. The curriculum of NYTS was biblically based, taking seriously the injunction of Jeremiah 29:7 — "promote the welfare of the city to which I have exiled you; pray for it to the LORD, for upon its welfare depends your own." That commitment and the fact that NYTS was deeply influenced by a theology of liberation provided strong motivation to develop a program at Sing Sing.

There were problems to overcome, but, as Paul suspected from the beginning, the problems had more to do with inevitable resistance on the part of the state correctional system than with NYTS's ability to adapt its program to a challenging new context without compromising academic quality and integrity. As he reflected about those years, one memory stood out — the action of the Board of Trustees. As was his pattern when proposing a new project to the board, Paul suggested that the trustees vote on the Sing Sing project with the proviso that it proceed only if money could be found. To his surprise, for the first and only time in his experience with them, the Board voted to go ahead with the program independently of whether there were sufficient funds on hand. They had confidence that the money would be found.

Fourteen years had passed since that meeting. Paul was now a past president serving on the NYTS faculty as professor of urban studies and director of the Sing Sing program. The program at Sing Sing had changed many lives. Of the 125 inmates who had earned the Master of Professional Studies degree, almost all were living productive lives on the outside. For example, Rodney Nelson, a graduate of the Sing Sing program, completed the M.Div. program at NYTS after his release and was now serving as pastor of a church in Harlem. Over the years, a few had returned to prison for minor parole violations but none for serious crime. The impact on the faculty was also important. One faculty member had recently spent a sabbatical visiting prisons in South Africa and Europe. He now taught a course about the criminal justice system. Students attending regular courses at NYTS were also influenced by the Sing Sing program. At least once each semester, a group of students made the trip "up the river" to spend an evening with their brothers on the inside.

Given the proliferation of its programs and the ever-growing needs of its constituencies, NYTS now found itself more beleaguered. The last thing needed was another program that would stretch the seminary's financial and human resources further. Economic disparity was growing between the large number of high-salaried people who either came into New York City to work or who lived in expensive city dwellings and those city dwellers who were unemployed or underemployed. New demands were being made on NYTS partner churches, a main source of financial support for the seminary. Social services that were in the past the responsibility of the government were falling to the churches. These financial pressures had major implications for the school. Of equal concern was the deteriorating quality of life of those who were most marginalized. The decline in social welfare had a direct impact on the life of the seminary, which was preparing leaders from the urban community for ministry within that community. The needs of the growing multicultural and multilingual student community and the urban churches were absorbing the energy and resources of the school.

It was in the face of these many challenges that Paul was about to propose the development of a new program at Sing Sing. The fact that the seminary already had an established program at the correctional institution did not necessarily make responding to this new situation any easier. In spite of the term "correctional," the prison system existed primarily to punish criminals. Although education had proven to be the most effective method of rehabilitation with lower recidivism for those who received education while in prison, in 1995 the state and federal governments withdrew all funds for college prison programs. When state and federal funding ceased, all of the accredited college programs withdrew their services. Most of the men who were admitted to the NYTS graduate program had earned their undergraduate degrees while incarcerated. Those who had graduated from the program knew the difference education made in their lives and the hope it gave them. They also understood the impact the lack of meaningful education would have on the prison environment. Prison at its best was a stressful place. Prison without hope and the positive influence of education could become a more dangerous place. It was with these concerns and to discuss alternatives that a group of ten inmate alums had come to meet with Paul that afternoon.

In conversation with the inmates and with the urging of Sing Sing's Superintendent, the highest official at that facility, an idea began to take shape. Paul became determined to propose that NYTS offer a college-level certificate for the inmates, using the graduates from the Master of Professional Studies program to assist with the teaching. The commitment of NYTS to Sing Sing was already a major one. Every semester six faculty members made the trip to Sing Sing each week as part of their regular faculty assignment. Paul taught two courses and spent an equivalent amount of time with the administration of the Sing Sing program. When needed, adjunct faculty were hired by the seminary. Expecting the faculty to take on additional responsibility at Sing Sing was unrealistic. On the other hand, Paul was convinced that engaging the inmates who had earned their master's degree as a resource for a certificate program would have a positive impact on them and possibly on their fellow inmates. But, would these inmates know how to teach? Even partnering them with civilian mentors would not necessarily guarantee good teaching. Even more significantly, how would the inmate population react to some inmates having status as teachers? Power struggles and "one-up-manship" were common among the inmates.

It was clear from Paul's conversations with Superintendent Peters that civilian involvement was essential for the program to succeed. The prison system would not deal with inmates as program decision makers. Would he be able to find civilian mentors? Then there were all the other practical difficulties of establishing another program. What department in the prison system would oversee it? Paul doubted that it would come under the prison chaplain as did the master's-level program. A college-level certificate would need to be linked to established education programs for an undergraduate college to be accredited. Where would the money come from to support a new program? The situation at Sing Sing and other state facilities warranted it, but . . .

Paul struggled with a dilemma. Should NYTS and other church-related institutions take on responsibilities that the government ought to assume, effectively letting the government "off the hook"? Perhaps it would be better to put energy into pushing the state to change its policies. He knew there was a need to fill the gap and to work for change. There were no easy answers. As these questions tumbled one after another in Paul's mind, the train pulled into Grand Central. Paul went up to the street level to walk the few blocks to the seminary. Once again he would be proposing that NYTS respond to the challenges created by a changing context. He smiled to himself and thought — so what else is new?

Background: Setting the Capitives Free
New York Theological Seminary

New York Theological Seminary (NYTS), begun in 1900 in New Jersey as an interdenominational Protestant Bible college, relocated in New York City in 1902. A critical turning point in the history of the institution was a change in the late 1960s. The seminary moved from a traditional residential program that trained pastors, teachers, and missionaries for service throughout the U.S. and the world, to an institution that specializes in educating lay and ordained men and women for urban parish ministry. NYTS has no residential students and employs experimental, contextual approaches to the education of church leaders in the metropolitan area, the vast majority of whom are Black, Hispanic, and Asian.

The seminary's theological diversity ranges from mainline Protestant to Pentecostal. At any one time there will be 48 to 50 denominations represented in the student body. At the time of this case study, the seminary's culturally and denominationally diverse faculty and student body, availability of multilingual programs (English, Korean, Spanish), variety of educational levels, advocacy for oppressed peoples, location in midtown Manhattan within a church building, and relatively low tuition rates all contributed to its distinction as "the most racially and culturally diverse seminary in America."[1]

To help address multicultural and multilingual diversity, both in the city and the seminary, all community seminary events are consciously focused on multilingual approaches. Groups distinguished by race, language, culture, and sexual orientation host worship and meals for the whole community. Students visit other students' churches and communities. The broad exposure to various cultures is intentional and central to the basic identity of the school.

Core faculty see the seminary as "grounded in the local context,"

---

1. Quoted passages come from official publications of the seminary and from interviews with seminary personnel.

which is defined by the distinctive ethnic makeup of New York City —
that is, by the marginalized communities of people of color: African
American, Korean, Hispanic, and Caribbean. Based on the conviction
that it is not possible to address the needs of the most blighted areas
without addressing issues of upscale areas, NYTS also includes in its
context suburban areas such as Westchester County. The seminary's
mission is to invest the more affluent with an awareness and concern
for the poor and to offer skills of social analysis, social action, and biblical faith to the poor to change their situation. The NYTS curriculum
is biblically based, oriented by liberation theologies, and shaped in dialogue with congregational partners. Faculty and administrators challenge regional and "urban" constituencies to address local issues
through greater understanding of social realities, ministry studies, and
community organizing. While some specific social issues such as welfare, AIDS, and poverty are addressed in elective courses, these and
other issues such as ecology are included in basic courses in Bible, theology, ethics, and ministry studies. Faculty members also work with
clusters of churches and design courses to address specific congregational needs and issues such as leadership development and team
building across religious traditions.

In recent years changes in the urban context have affected NYTS's
partner congregations and consequently the seminary's mission, goals,
and programs. A collective depression in the economic, moral, and social climate has meant that the struggles of people who are most
marginalized have either remained the same or become worse. In the
last several years, the churches with which the seminary works are being
pressed to deliver more than other agencies and organizations in order
to address the quality of life of their constituents. Coupled with national, state, and local cutbacks, there are few, if any, restorative zones
to draw upon. Students bring this crisis into the classrooms.

Primary issues raised by seminary constituents and addressed in
elective courses and in the integrated focus on social theory and analysis include:

1. *Community building.* How can the church build a new human community in light of the decline of social welfare?
2. *Attention to justice issues without entering the "charity trap."* Courses
   draw clearly on liberation theologies. Faculty seek "a transforma-

59

tive Christian witness that has broad application to the economy, political commitments, and the family."

3. *Empowering disempowered people.* This topic is addressed specifically in biblical studies, ethics, and mission and ministry courses. The particular strategies suggested are dependent on the person, context, and analysis of how power is taken from people, and on working in collaboration with others about how the gospel calls people to empowerment.

At the time of this case study, NYTS offered three degree programs and a certificate program. The Master of Professional Studies was originally designed for leaders in the historic Black denominations and the emerging Pentecostal Church, for whom ordination did not require formal theological education. In recent years, students see the MPS as a way of exploring theological education. A distinctive component of this degree program is offered for long-term prisoners at Sing Sing Correctional Facility. Students must have completed an accredited bachelor's degree and be willing to undertake a demanding combination of academic and field work. Sing Sing students pay no tuition for this program, which is fully supported by gifts and grants to the seminary.

The Master of Divinity is a standard graduate degree for professional, ordained ministry in North America. Those admitted must have a B.A. or equivalent degree from an accredited four-year college and have a base in a specific congregation where they are involved in lay or clerical activities. The Doctor of Ministry is a three-year interdisciplinary degree offered in English, Korean, and Spanish. This program is self-consciously interfaith and includes Jewish rabbis and Muslims as participants.

Of an average 320 participants in these combined programs, some 47 percent are Black, 30 percent Asian, 12 percent Hispanic, and 11 percent White. Sixty percent of these participants are men and 40 percent are women. Faculty members are committed to maintaining a solid constituency of Whites, which has averaged from 18 to 20 percent over the past 15 years. Sixty percent of NYTS students are over 40 years old.

The Certificate in Christian Ministry is a two-year program designed for women and men with a high school diploma or equivalent who desire to be more effective in their ministries. Students who successfully complete this program can receive eight transfer credits toward a bachelor's degree at the College of New Rochelle. Of an average number of 150 certificate students, the majority are Black and Hispanic.

Within the faculty, composed of 14 core faculty, 12 associates, and 18 adjuncts, there is a broad diversity of African-American, White, and Asian men and women, with fewer Hispanics. While compatibility with the current faculty is important, the primary criterion used in selecting new faculty for NYTS is commitment to the mission of the seminary and commitment to local church ministries. The faculty and administration value racial and gender diversity above denominational diversity. Faculty affirm that the most effective teaching approach to prepare program participants for urban ministry is an interactive style that uses small groups and plenary discussions, and draws on the rich life experiences of course participants. All faculty appointments at every level are approved by the core faculty. Specific faculty-training programs in teaching approaches take place on retreats for adjunct and core faculty.

NYTS gives priority to partner relationships with church communities and leaders within the metropolitan New York area. The seminary has also forged long-standing partner relationships with General Theological Seminary (Episcopalian) and Union Theological Seminary (interdenominational), both located in New York City. This partnership includes cross-registration with both schools. In addition, through collaborative planning, it is possible for students to earn the Master of Social Work degree from Fordham University or the Master of Arts degree in urban studies from Queens College (City University of New York) while working on the Master of Divinity degree.

Discussion Notes: Setting the Captives Free

Teaching Goals on Constituency and Contextualization

- To explore the meaning of contextualization in urban ministry for constituents, practitioners, and educators
- To explore the implications of a challenge in a new mission field that stretches limited human and financial resources
- To consider the theological implications for individual faculty and institutions as they move to clarify calling and set institutional priorities in a contextualized program for urban ministry
- To explore the obligations and limitations of church and state to meet social needs

Discussion Questions

1. How does NYTS's understanding of its context as "urban" shape its mission and ministry? What informs the priorities of a faith-based institution in reference to special needs, such as the inmates at Sing Sing?

2. In a critical analysis of the needs of an urban population, what problems stand out? How might you both advise and collaborate with the pastors, educators, and urban advocates of NYTS?

3. What are the specific implications of the biblical mandate to "promote the welfare of the city" for NYTS? What are the implications and mandates for your own ministry and constituency?

4. What is the line between government responsibility for social rehabilitation and the theological mandate to serve the poor and those in prison? Explore the demands of compassion and justice.

Role-Play

Structure a contextual role-play between Alex and Pastor John. Alex is a Sing Sing inmate who has just completed his master's degree through NYTS. He is a strong proponent of NYTS's establishing a college program at Sing Sing and has volunteered to teach. Pastor John is a member of the NYTS board of trustees. He believes NYTS is already over-extended. John thinks NYTS should celebrate its current ministry at Sing Sing, but is hesitant to enter into a college program because, "This is not what seminaries do."

After five to ten minutes of the role-play in a "fish bowl" setting, de-role the players and ask participants to share their insights from this interchange at the emotional and intellectual level.

What are the implications of the role-play for a congregation or institution that is being challenged to take its ministry outside traditional parameters?

Alternative Discussion Questions

The following alternative approach was developed by Stanley Saunders, Columbia Theological Seminary, and Sue Zabel, Wesley Theological Seminary. It focuses on prison ministry and draws on biblical texts and the rich personal experiences of participants.

1. Ask participants to share their experiences (or lack) in ministry within prisons.

2. Explore in small groups (2-3 persons) a range of biblical texts pertinent to ministry in prisons.

3. Review with the full group the Christian tradition of ministry within prison settings.

4. Discuss the current situation with regard to America's exploding prison population and the "Prison Industrial Complex."

5. Discuss the pros and cons of Paul's case for NYTS. Push participants for the theological implications of their positions.

6. Register participants' (pro-con) views as to whether NYTS should pursue the new program. Discuss the rationales for positions taken.

7. Identify and discuss constituencies in the urban setting that are parallel to the prison population.

8. Identify alternatives and resources for NYTS and other institutions seeking to enter this type of ministry.

Application Exercise

Ask each person to write a prayer of no more than five lines for a liberating ministry to the city. Invite those who desire to share their prayers in a plenary session. What resources are reflected in these prayers? What are the implications of these prayers for action in urban ministry?

Suggestions for Specific Group Discussion

For practitioners such as pastors, theological students, and urban advocates, focus on goals one, two, and four and questions two, three, and four.

For representatives of seminary faculties or trustees, funding agencies or denominational representatives, focus on goals one, two, and three and questions one, three, and four.

Either group would benefit from following the alternative set of questions.

Commentary

MICHAEL A. MATA

The urban context of contemporary ministry argues for a different kind of engagement in ministry preparation than those traditional approaches to theological education adopted by most seminaries. The case studies show that both the C. P. Haggard Graduate School of Theology (HGST) at Azusa Pacific University and New York Theological Seminary (NYTS) are attempting to take seriously the urban landscape where most of their students live, work, and minister. In the process, both schools have been challenged to reconfigure themselves as institutions of theological education to the contours of the terrain. While NYTS has been at it longer, and in many ways more effectively, than HGST, both face significant hurdles to having vital and viable contextualized programs.

The process of contextualization entails a profound appreciation for the urban environment. The stories of NYTS and HGST underscore the notion that the lens adopted to gauge the social realities does affect the development of relevant curriculum and appropriate pedagogy. For NYTS, whose location in the city affords its leadership a keen perspective on New York urban life, the urban community struggles with social, economic, and physical decline. More significant, the so-called suburbs are not immune, in the eyes of the NYTS leadership, to the effects of this deterioration; there is no real urban-suburban dichotomy here. Thus, the curriculum at NYTS challenges and equips the entire Christian community, regardless of its social or geographic location, to confront the socio-economic realities in tangible and hope-filled ways.

On the other hand, HGST emphasizes the ethnic heterogeneity and multicultural character of the ever-changing Los Angeles context. Not discounting the effects of the devolution of government programs, the demographic profiles of its constituencies demand language-specific tracks and diversified educational programs. Its curriculum tends to help students work more effectively within their specific con-

65

text rather than gain a broader or more comprehensive understanding of ministry in the urban context. At the same time, with the concentration of people of color in the urban core and the financial support coming from white suburban churches, there is a real cultural divide for HGST between urban and suburban.

These different notions of the city shape the nature of the primary problems raised in each case. For NYTS the challenge is between being responsive to the needs of the churches as they attempt to address the issues of urban life, and being a responsible institution in terms of its resources: How can an institution in solidarity with churches of the city be sensitive in its program development to the diverse needs of its constituency and at the same time be able to sustain itself? This is probably *THE* issue for vital and viable urban leadership development. The needs of contemporary urban life far outweigh the resources of any one institution or organization. The struggle to remain relevant is not new to NYTS, nor will that challenge go away — even if the school becomes blessed with adequate financial resources. This "problem" is by definition the crucible of contextualized urban theological education, particularly when the city is perceived as a place wrought with socio-economic problems and few or diminishing assets.

In the case of HGST, bridging the urban-suburban divide has been problematic even when there have been sufficient resources and a legitimate attempt to be part of the physical landscape of the city. The geographic distance between the source of resources and the delivery of services (i.e., courses and mentoring) heightens the cultural gulf between the main leadership of the school and the students' urban reality: When does an institution that sees itself as taking its resources "into" the city become part of the urban context? There are real differences in providing education "to, in, and with." This raises a significant issue in regard to the meaning and process of contextualization.

The case of NYTS highlights the notion that contextualized theological education can mean being *RESPONSIVE* to the needs and struggles of its constituencies. Theological education for NYTS in this instance is not an enterprise done in isolation from urban life — in some "ivory tower" — but one that strives to be rooted in the experiences of its church supporters. Its commitment to the context, then, is reflected in the content and venues of its curriculum and programs. The process at times appears to be more organic than academic. As such, it is time intensive and built on the quality of relationships established among all the stakeholders — e.g., church leaders, students (both clergy and lay), faculty members, school administrators, and other educational institutions. This is not your conventional approach to program development. For HGST, contextualized education seems to be about respecting the cultural makeup of its constituency. In this case it is about making its curriculum *ACCESSIBLE* to its ethnically and linguistically diverse student body. While the physical context and life experiences of the students may find their way serendipitously into course content, HGST is focused on adapting an established curriculum to a highly heterogeneous constituency. This also is time intensive. Both cases point to the fact that contextualized education mandates a certain level of risk and experimentation, especially to find the right balance between resources and needs. When it comes to managing the process of contextualization, there are also other differences and similarities in both of these experiences.

These differences and similarities emerge between the schools as they try to address the challenge of contextualization. Both NYTS and HGST have invested their respective resources into program development rather than physical infrastructure. The latter, of course, limits some programmatic development, but by partnering with other churches and parachurch institutions both schools provide different venues for learning as well as learning experiences. Non-residential programs allow for this kind of flexibility. The lack of extensive permanent facilities also frees up funds for scholarships. Both schools are highly invested in procuring additional funds to enable limited-income and underrepresented students to enroll in their respective programs. The danger, especially for HGST whose scholarship program is grant-driven, is how to plan for the drying up of scholarship resources.

The strength of any program, of course, will lie in its faculty. Of the two schools, NYTS has the most diverse and experienced faculty; they reflect the community and are comfortable in the context. That is not the case for HGST. While the leadership of the urban program has challenged the faculty of the school to engage the context, it is still foreign to most. A concerted effort has been made to recruit adjunct faculty members, as NYTS has done as well, more in tune with its students' life and ministry experiences. The situations of both schools demonstrate that bridging the gulf between formal educational structures, wherever they are based, and the demands of a highly complex and rich environment like the city is resource intensive. There is no way of getting around this fact, especially when there are other concerns vying for attention. The task of identifying the crucial resources is an ever-present challenge to any committed institution.

Although the two situations reflect different approaches to contextualization, they both underscore that there must exist a high level of commitment by the institution to the context. The very nature of context suggests that the manner of carrying out its institutional commitment will vary from time to time. Change in demographics or ethnicity is a case in point. More important, as the case of NYTS well demonstrates, that commitment must be lifted up constantly. It is not a matter of simply having the commitment articulated in a mission statement. Both schools have someone in leadership who is knowledgeable about the urban context and committed to it. These individuals in both instances have been bridge-builders in that they have focused their energies and skills on narrowing the chasm between administration and faculty and their intended constituency. This is not an easy task; there are those who are resistant to change or fearful of change. In other words, these kinds of bridge-building individuals are instrumental in garnering and maintaining support for the urban programs. It is hopeful to note that in the case of NYTS, as the internal evidence suggests, it is a Euro-American who has been the ever-present advocate for the city. While HGST has a Latino to guide the process, the case of NYTS demonstrates that it is not essential that the head be a person of color.

What is essential is that the educational institution becomes a learning organization. As the NYTS case shows, a learning environment is one that allows for innovation. This means a high level of trust for the person or persons initiating the changes and allowing for some failures as well. This attitude is critical if an innovative program is instituted — whether that means offering courses in a non-English language or leading degree-oriented seminars in prison. Following these experiences, the learning institution makes adjustments and adapts or recognizes the need for additional resources or skills. In both case studies, the institutions forged their urban programs upon their resident assets, namely, their instructors. While NYTS has experimented with developing new pedagogical methods, HGST still has some distance to

68

go. Nonetheless, an institution that wants to be contextually relevant must invest in developing a cadre of equipped and experienced learning facilitators, either through re-education of current faculty members or recruitment of new instructors.

It is clear that the issue of sustainability is looming. Administratively, a program that drains resources will be short-lived or, as soon as the additional resources disappear, the program will be downsized or restructured. Both case studies mention the forging of partnerships with other entities. Collaboration is not only crucial to viable urban programs as a way to share the costs, but points to the fact that critical resources already exist in the city. In other words, the city is not devoid of assets. In fact, part of the retooling of urban theological education must include learning to identify the resident resources with which God has endowed the city. For example, NYTS has had a long-running relationship with the urban church community, and HGST has partnered with a long-standing parachurch organization. Other dimensions of contextualization may entail cultivating new kinds of resources.

If contextualization means appreciating the urban context as a viable locus for learning and ministry rich with resources, it suggests embracing the context in its totality — not only its problems and pathologies but also its potential. To embrace the total context includes being able to read the text of the urban landscape as to its history and current state of affairs, and perhaps glimpse its future. This ability to read the text may steer the course of theological education away from reactive or adaptive modes of contextualization to one that intentionally explores the edges of ministry and engages in entrepreneurial forms of education. In "Setting the Captive Free" the primary actor, Paul, appears to be doing just that. Conventional thinking would recommend "go with your strengths; partner and facilitate the program rather than take it on." But Paul seems poised to uncover a whole new and even more challenging understanding of contextualization. He will certainly need to invest some time in guiding his colleagues through the new path of engagement.

In "Another World" Carlos may have a sense of that challenge, but for now he must be content with helping his faculty find comfort and hope in what they have been able to accomplish. The program is relatively young compared to that of NYTS. Whereas the urban program of

NYTS is wholly its own program, HGST's urban program is only part of a larger enterprise. However, Carlos can cultivate and nurture a learning environment that could embolden current and future faculty to fully embrace the city and its future.

Commentary

CAROLYN TENNANT

The incarnation of Christ in the city. The church at work in the urban context. What would Jesus do today? Amid all that could be done, where would he start? One fact is certain: He would not remove himself from the center of the action. He hung out where it was uncomfortable and confronted the system. He turned tables and lives upside down. We learn a lot about people when we discover what makes them unhappy, and so we should consider this: Jesus wept over the city. Shouldn't we as Christian educators react in the same way?

Perhaps the most gripping story of the last century is that a large number of churches, along with Christian educational institutions, simply packed up and left the cities. Many removed themselves from the action when city life got too hot. They took off with more than material goods; they took along some salt and light. Others didn't leave; they simply chose never to enter the urban context in the first place. These sorts of decisions by Christians have contributed to almost insurmountable problems of context and constituencies. They are at the core of many questions like these:

1. If faculty have not experienced the realities of urban life, how can they effectively teach others what it means to live as Christian transformers in a societal context that in all honesty they do not really understand?

2. Are general principles of leadership sufficient when taught to urban dwellers from a suburban perspective? Are there inherent differences in these two worlds that mandate that leadership must also be different? If so, exactly how?

3. Without a presence in the city, many seminaries have produced fewer leaders of diversity and urban experience who are educationally prepared to address the present urban challenges. The potential leaders often did not have the money, the transportation, or the gumption to attend seminaries or Christian colleges in the suburbs. Now we are

71

reaping the fruits of this neglect in that we cannot find sufficient trained faculty with contextualized urban experience. What, then, do we do to provide quality instruction that adequately addresses the complexity of the multilingual, multicultural, multireligious, multiethnic, multiracial, and multivalued society that composes our present urban sprawls?

4. Without the realities of fairly substantial urban experiences, myths and misunderstandings about the urban context are likely to abound. These mitigate against the comfortability of both relationship and application that are important for good learning. How can we overcome this hurdle?

Indeed, there are deep challenges inherent in offering truly contextualized education to the great variety of urban constituencies. Many of the problems extend to the root of who we are. The world around us has changed and is mandating that we reconsider our mission statements in light of these changes.

The mission of C. P. Haggard Graduate School of Theology (HGST), for example, is a straightforward one: to prepare people for effective practical ministry in the church throughout the world. The challenge for many seminaries and Christian schools of higher education is that our mission statements meant one thing thirty years ago and have entirely different implications now. The "world" has changed! Diversity, urbanization, globalization, information technology, and extensive issues of justice are only some of the shifts that have occurred. In order to prepare ministers for our world, as it truly is today, we have to change. For HGST, "effective practical ministry" in the urban context is a huge challenge. The church in the urban world needs increasingly complex and sophisticated skills in order to do its job. Will Haggard and others of us be able to change sufficiently to meet these needs?

It would be easier if institutional change did not mandate some very personal rearrangements. It can take us past our comfort zones. Faced with challenges such as those noted in the earlier questions, both Haggard and New York Theological Seminary (NYTS) now have to find ways of helping faculty to understand a constantly changing urban context. NYTS has to work within the shifting needs of a prison system. Haggard is being called upon to acquire insight into different cultural mores, into various ways of perceiving the world, and into an unfamiliar reality. Its faculty has to bear new inconveniences (lack of parking can be a hot concern!) and possible safety issues. They are stretched to learn cross-culturally and then teach cross-culturally. Content must be reconsidered, but so must teaching methodologies. Faculties need to relearn and rethink, to become personally vulnerable. If this does not continually occur at HGST, NYTS, and other schools attempting to provide education in the urban centers, then they will undoubtedly see some ramifications. Although there has been an increase over the past years in older students and commuters as well as ethnic students at Haggard, if education should ever appear "not applicable to our world," then it is likely that the enrollment of those particular constituencies will decline. Faculty must enter the present urban context not only to teach but also to become involved there in interactive learning among its various groups. Can education be truly viable and alive in any other way?

A related problem of faculty development faces New York Theological Seminary since the present number of faculty does not appear to be sufficient to handle additional degree-level courses. Will NYTS be able to develop its graduates from the Sing Sing program so that they are sufficiently prepared to teach in the new prison program? The institution is again being required to stretch, retool, and find new patterns in regard to faculty. One could perhaps say that it should not have to be NYTS's responsibility to develop undergraduate learning opportunities. However, the inability to find a solution to this particular problem will sooner or later affect the health of the entire master's program and its services to this special constituency.

How NYTS chooses to resolve this problem should also extend from a re-examination of its mission statement. If it is not within the mission statement of the seminary to provide for quality undergraduate certification, then perhaps a response can be found by partnering with an undergraduate institution with a heart for this ministry. The challenge does not lie simply in persuading the government to fund undergraduate education, but rather in persuading biblical undergraduate institutions to find creative solutions to continue their services even without such funding. They need to be called to fulfill their Christian responsibility and to meet the challenges inherent in their own mission statements! Faith must enter the economic picture at all educational levels.

On the other hand, the problem may still end up at the door of

NYTS. A model for handling the dilemma of servicing constituencies without undergraduate degrees has been effectively developed by the Center for Urban Ministerial Education, the Boston branch of Gordon-Conwell Theological Seminary. It was a challenge to find ways of handling this problem at the seminary level, but CUME has proved that there are feasible solutions. I would like to encourage NYTS to consider similar creative options and try jumping some new hurdles.

Although New York Theological Seminary has come a long way in responding to its context, it will be important for it to keep growing and changing. How much change is enough? Since society is experiencing shifts in political, economic, and demographic structures, a growing institution has to be ready to make changes to meet these new needs. It cannot settle into the old patterns, or it will lose its earlier success at contextualization. Just such a challenge faces NYTS in this decision regarding its prison ministry. This institution has worked so hard on contextualization in the past that it has been a model to many of us. We trust that it will be able to stay on that cutting edge, not just regarding this issue but other ones which will inevitably come its way. Ongoing, nonstop change needs to become a reality for all of us.

Our academic world can become too comfortable, too predictable: a kind of virtual reality shooting gallery in which we respond within computer-generated space, acting as if it is reality. In this environment, we can trip over things, jerk in response, move forward or backward. There's just one problem. It's not the real world.

As the academic dean at North Central University, I have noticed that our institution's location in the city center of Minneapolis has forced continuous challenges to our thinking and implications for our curriculum. We recently revamped every major in one year . . . not an easy task, I will have to admit. However, we were motivated by the shifts in our context and in the constituencies that we serve. We were determined to do a better job of serving, and with that in mind, the task even became fun. I would like to encourage HGST and NYTS to consider their necessary shifts as ones of growth and joy rather than fear and pain. At NCU we are finding that the urban context can be a place of mutual growth and learning for students and faculty alike. It stretches everyone — sometimes even to the point of uneasiness and frustration, but we have come to love the learning lab which is around us.

As those of us in academia have to grapple with a context that is constantly in flux, the new game plan and "rules" may well make us un-comfortable. However, we have to decide whose uncomfortability it is going to be. Will we make the students come to us and try to fit into our world, or will we work at becoming enmeshed in theirs? As challenging as the answer is, I believe that an incarnational Christ would do the latter. It is costly service, but Christian educators are called to the cross. Besides, it wouldn't be so costly now if we hadn't neglected our diverse urban fields in the first place.

Christ is undoubtedly challenging us today in Christian higher education. Are we willing to get involved in the city itself and work on behalf of the *shalom* of the city — or will we remain comfortable in the safety of our present existence? The answer is not one to be considered lightly. The challenges need to be faced not simply by HGST and NYTS. These schools are to be congratulated for grappling with the issues! We all need to consider honestly the state of higher education within our greater world context today.

Generally speaking, education tends to program students for a society that no longer exists — a simpler, static, non-urbanized society. The academy has not changed rapidly enough, but in some ways this is understandable. There is such an exponential increase in knowledge coupled with the compaction of the world with its many complicated facets! How can we possibly keep up even in our own fields, let alone the broader fields of interdisciplinary education? After all, the concept of the well-rounded, broadly educated "Renaissance man" slipped from our fingers a long time ago. However, with the massive changes in society, we can no longer remain satisfied teaching the same lectures within the same four walls of academia.

Christian higher education has to face the actual world of urbanization and ethnic/cultural/racial change that is occurring. If we want to survive, contextualization isn't an option; it is a mandate. When we do not adjust our teaching as society shifts around us, then education becomes increasingly dysfunctional. If schools insist on retaining their traditional forms in the face of massive societal changes, they will doom themselves to obsolescence and decline. We must force ourselves to grapple in a profound way with the real-world context.

We cannot ignore the fact that dysfunctionalism is actually occurring in traditional education when we consider some signs: arguments about an educational voucher system, the sharp increase in home schooling and private schooling options, on-line education, distance education, and higher education choices through institutes and parachurch organizations. The urban context is no stranger to these alternative forms of education, but it adds another — the dropout, the disenfranchised, the disenchanted. Surely Christian education has a way of speaking to these. This is why NYTS needs to consider carefully how it will keep serving the real needs of the prison population.

It is no longer possible to pretend that society is like it was fifty, thirty, or even ten years ago. It is improbable that we will be able to keep doing business as usual. If we do not change, then new models will rise up in our place. NYTS seemed to know this much earlier than most of us. It realized it needed to change, and its crisis came thirty years ago. It is useful to have a model with a track record of change. The very roots of the institution were in the urban context. It stayed in a church building, and it thrives from church-based funding and support. Everything is located where the people are involved in their daily lives. The faculty is composed of a large number of individuals who not only understand the people but also *are* the people. However, will NYTS realize that there are brand-new needs and problems, and will they determine to respond to those?

Although it is in comparatively early stages of change, Haggard Graduate School of Theology also faced the challenge and determined to provide "an incarnational ministry to the urban context" through the opening of its Urban Center. However, the shift of a primarily suburban faculty to a context in which they are not presently located presents some real challenges. It is difficult to know how to confront, respond to, and work with strong urban systems when one has not lived and worked in them. HGST faculty should consider moving their homes into the context in which they are dedicated to teach. Furthermore, transforming these systems becomes even more challenging. How does one speak *shalom* in a strange context? It is not impossible to do, but it is very challenging. True *shalom* means not so much doing something *to* or *for* people, but rather doing it *with* them and empowering them to do it for themselves in the future. Experience and deep understanding are needed to do this effectively.

From experience with our urban school, I can say that just because a school is located in an urban center does not mean that it will automatically fare better. Even though schools may be in the heart of an urban context, they can be largely unaware of and remain blissfully untouched by the world around them. The glass bubble can provide an effective shelter. Students can trip over drunks on their way to class and only be irritated or full of pity. Either way, the end result can be the same. No action. What we all have to do is to wake up to the real world around us NOW and decide what that means to our own comfortable world. It takes a stretch, a change, both personally and corporately.

Our case institutions are facing specific problems regarding effectual service to their urban constituencies. For example, HGST may at times be perceived by its urban students to lack administrative friendliness. Its main campus is far away, and access to the library — a learning basic — is not easy. Serving the student may mean that regular van runs could be made to the main campus or car-pooling services could be organized. Extra personnel may be needed to bring registration and other administrative functions to the students at off hours, rather than expecting the students to take off from work simply to get to the main campus during the day. There will undoubtedly be a financial hurdle to such services that will challenge the seminary, but since it is determined to serve urban people, this may well be part of the price.

We must decide how far we are willing to spread our finances in order to underwrite vision. Limited resources have a way of revealing true values. They can also bring out faith and creativity. Sometimes lack of resources is an excuse for inaction, but we need to measure our commitment to contextualization and to various constituencies by how hard we try to overcome the resource barrier that we all face.

We also need to move past naïveté and shock when it comes to learning a new cultural constituency such as those in a prison context (NYTS) or a diverse inner-city world (HGST). With the changing demographics that are the norm in our society, it is time to discover processes that will engage us in constant relearning in these areas. Recently during an in-service day at North Central University, I loaded all of the faculty on a bus, and we drove around our neighborhood for an hour observing the changing people, shops, housing, and religious services. I looked back at one point and noticed tears streaming down a couple of faces, and several more were just shaking their heads. They concluded that we need to do this tour regularly. Changes in the curriculum came forth immediately.

We also have tremendous challenges regarding curriculum development. When a suburban faculty identifies the greatest needs for urban pastors/leaders without including their perspective, how can we be sure the resulting program will meet the real needs of the population? Such challenges become even greater when considering the demands of special populations like NYTS's Sing Sing prisoners. Some of our greatest contributions to our students come when we give them a voice. We need to let them help us design useful learning experiences — to let practitioners and alumni have a hand in the actual development of the curriculum.

As we listen to our constituency groups tell us what their true needs are, it can change our learning sets. We have to find out what people want to know. We must then do the hard work of finding ways to empower them to handle the nitty-gritty problems of their world such as economic disparity, social injustice, and the political system. If we don't know, then let's learn the answers together — students and faculty joined in discovering God's approach to the present society. The old paradigm is that the faculty needs to be the dispenser of knowledge. That perspective must change so that it enfolds curiosity, learning together, assessing, discovering solutions, and working through processes.

Frequently we do not understand difficulties, needs, and real pain without some discovery, but we probably also do not comprehend the joys of the urban context — even the potentially positive points of prison rehabilitation. Short views provide a picture of huge problems and needs. But actually living there expands one's view to include celebration, victories, and God-sightings. God is already at work in these contexts!

It is also easy to miss the fact that various cultures view their constituencies in a different light. Some, for example, have a most positive view of women in leadership. Each school must decide how it will relate to the 51 percent of the population through whom God is working in the city, namely women. A lack of women teaching in the core classes at Haggard, for example, will undoubtedly affect the perceived leadership ability of the female learners. There is probably a lack of trained women faculty for all of the same reasons that there is a lack of trained urban leaders of various ethnic backgrounds. Overcoming this problem will demand much creativity and work.

At NYTS, the considerable number of women faculty attests the importance of women in home, work, and church. Not surprisingly, this is reflected in the student enrollment. Various ethnic, racial, and cultural groups are likewise represented both in the faculty and in the student body. The Body of Christ is composed of many, and a community that does not reflect this diversity is in need. It's in need of more joy, more learning, more growth.

Issues involving constituencies abound in the urban context. About two-thirds of Haggard's total faculty are Caucasian; thus, they may have challenges understanding the wide range of cultural, ethnic, and racial diversity. Serving diverse student groups will demand sensitivity on the part of instructors to various learning styles, classroom behavior, multiple expectations, and varied experiences. This reveals the need for teacher training, yet another commitment in time, energy, and finances.

If we are to make a difference to the people of the city, we have to do more than go to a place simply because we are curious. We also can't do it to assuage our consciences or to provide good public relations. God help us not to do the job incompletely or with limited quality. No, it is not possible to do a "hit and run" job when it comes to urban relationships. I don't believe God would be particularly satisfied with Christian education that threw in some books but didn't change the world. God's plan is much more pervasive. Co-learning and personal transformation, vulnerability and personal stretch: these are the demands of our times. When we take up the challenge, it is likely we will come out of it renewed and invigorated. God help us stay in the life-changing business!

Case Study: Service and Survival

Donald Gardner leaned back in his chair and looked out the window of the recently renovated house that served as the administrative offices for CUTS, Center for Urban Theological Studies. In the twilight descending over Hunting Park, several prostitutes were already lined up across the street. Don contemplated the upcoming meeting with CUTS's academic dean and the president, who began his tenure in 1994. Don planned to present the next steps for pursuing accreditation of CUTS's own courses and programs, a move he was convinced would insure CUTS's future.

A student appeared at his open door and interrupted Don's work. "Can you help me? The Financial Aid Office closed at 5 P.M., and I need help with this application form before I go over to the academic center for my classes." Don responded, as he always did, "Pull up a chair. Show me the problem."

Forty-five minutes later, Don returned to the meeting's agenda and wondered how CUTS could survive all the recent changes and still uphold its mission. He thought to himself, "Our dilemma is meeting the needs of the urban church while keeping CUTS alive and doing the things necessary to keep us open."

This case was written by Youtha Hardman-Cromwell and Sue Zabel. The names of all persons, with the exception of historical figures, have been disguised to protect the privacy of the individuals involved.

The Birth of CUTS

As he tried to refocus on the agenda, Don reflected on the history of CUTS. In the 1970s, urban pastors in Philadelphia sought training to help them meet the unique challenges of urban ministry. Most of these pastors were bi-vocational, full-time ministers who worked full-time in secular employment. Most did not need a seminary degree for ordination, yet they wanted a theologically sound education, grounded in street-level practicality, to help them cope with the rapidly changing needs of the city.

A majority of the urban pastors interested in additional theological education did not have undergraduate degrees and were unable to enroll in accredited seminary courses. In 1971, informal seminars and later a non-degree diploma program known as the Westminster Ministerial Institute (WMI) were developed at Westminster Theological Seminary, located in a Philadelphia suburb, to meet some of their needs. In 1978, through a partnership with Geneva College, WMI became the Center for Urban Theological studies and began to offer accredited undergraduate courses from its new base in Philadelphia. Since urban pastors were bi-vocational, undergraduate degrees served them not only in their ministerial training but also in vocational training.

Don remembered that in the beginning no educational institutions in Philadelphia offered regionally accredited ministry and theological training, and no seminaries offered programs during the evening. CUTS offered the first undergraduate and master's-level ministry training that was accessible to students who could not afford to leave daytime employment and to African-American pastors who were disenfranchised by the predominantly white schools in the area. CUTS soon became even more focused on its niche — those denied a theological education primarily due to the lack of prior educational experience — and designed courses for students who needed a GED and a solid foundation in basic education, such as writing skills.

Donald Gardner clearly recalled his coming to CUTS. His urban congregation, Christian Stronghold Baptist Church, pastored by Dr. Willie Richardson, sent and financially supported Donald to work as a layperson to help launch the organization. Nearly twenty years later, he still felt that burning passion for CUTS and urban ministries. He thought about the many hats he had worn as vice president: oversight of the academic programs, student services, computer development, funding, and personnel.

Evolving Identity and Mission

When CUTS was established, 90 percent of its students were Philadelphia pastors seeking to increase their knowledge and skills in urban ministry. Currently, the student body consisted of lay and clergy persons in ministry. One-third of the students were persons serving congregations as pastors; two-thirds were enrolled in classes to prepare for secular employment. CUTS's evolving mission reflected its commitment to provide accessible education for non-traditional students.

In order to respond to the changing urban environment and encompass lay education, social goals, and continuing education for clergy, CUTS's current mission statement included a commitment to:

- Provide education, training, and resources to develop servant-leaders for the urban church, community, and marketplace;
- Serve the needs of Christian adult learners and church leadership, helping them assess personal values, enhance ministry skills, develop interpersonal skills, and enhance professional competencies in order to influence the quality of work within their ministries and secular organizations, for the betterment of the overall community.

Don was reminded of one high school dropout who came to CUTS, completed his GED and undergraduate work, and went on to complete a Ph.D. This student was one of the many who wanted educational degrees to prepare for economically viable careers that complement ordained and lay ministries in congregations. He thought, "If Christians are to positively impact this sin-sick world, it is imperative that we gain strategic access to influential positions."

Partnerships and Educational Brokering:
A CUTS Innovation

As Don assessed where CUTS stood in its ability to attract and serve students, he was aware that it now competed with other institutions for non-traditional students. Throughout its history, CUTS served the educational needs of urban churches and communities through pioneering a series of partnerships that allowed CUTS to broker non-credit courses and accredited educational programs that responded to the changing needs of the urban community.

Don reflected on the nature of CUTS's institutional relationships. In 1978, Geneva College agreed to offer through CUTS a bachelor's program for urban church leaders in the greater Philadelphia area. In 1981, Westminster Theological Seminary offered the M.A.R. (Master of Arts in Religion) degree to urban church leadership through CUTS. Bill Krispin, CUTS's Executive Director until 1994, developed policies to equalize the partnerships with these two larger and more financially solvent schools. CUTS took the initiative in program development and raised funds for new programs.

In Bill Krispin's words, the very essence of brokering was "working to bring strengths together for the benefit of a constituency that heretofore has been disenfranchised." Don believed that one of the strengths CUTS brought to the partnership was recognizing the value of on-the-job training on a par with traditional classroom instruction. While he felt that this central tenet of CUTS courses brought difficulties to the partnership, and paternalistic attitudes remained, he quickly reminded himself that "without Westminster and Geneva's commitment, there would be no CUTS as we know it."

Now some twenty years after its birth, CUTS collaborated with Geneva College to offer five degree programs: B.S. in Urban Ministry Leadership, A.A. in Biblical Studies, B.S. in Bible and Ministry, B.S. in Human Resources, and B.S. in Human Services. Classes were held in CUTS's academic center, located several blocks from the administrative building and leased from the Roman Catholic Archdiocese of Philadelphia. CUTS also worked in partnership with Westminster Theological Seminary to offer a Master of Arts in Urban Mission degree. The CUTS staff oversaw the contextual, practical, and on-site learning requirements of this degree.

Don was enthusiastic about the CUTS Board of Trustees' investigation of another unprecedented cooperative venture. The presidents of three area colleges had recently met with CUTS's president and proposed the formation of a CUTS Christian Junior College. All three colleges had an interest in urban ministry education but were located outside Philadelphia's boundaries. Their predominantly white student bodies had few opportunities to learn about ministry in the city. CUTS's predominantly ethnic students would be able to enroll in accredited programs that previously seemed inaccessible. Graduates of the junior college would be able to continue their education at one of the three sponsoring schools or through one of CUTS's other adult education programs. In addition, the administration was exploring new off-site locations for classes in corporate facilities for job-related degree programs in human services and resources, which could bring courses to an even broader constituency. One of CUTS's strategic goals was to double enrollment in the next three to five years.

Strengths to Build On

Don was proud of CUTS's accomplishments. More than 500 graduates had received accredited degrees through CUTS's partnership with Geneva and Westminster. Most of them now served churches in the Philadelphia area. CUTS's 1999 summer enrollment was the highest ever. Enrollment in all programs ranged between 175 to 200 students, fairly evenly divided between African-American men and women. The student body now also included a small number of Asian and Hispanic students.

From the beginning, CUTS had been accountable to the churches and community by responding quickly and flexibly to the changing needs of urban churches and communities. Don recalled telling the dean not long ago, "CUTS is 'ground up,' not 'top down.' The local church decides who its leaders are. Our job is to help them become more efficient in whatever ministry God has called them to." While he had referred to leaders who had come up through the ranks of congregations, Don was aware that, more recently, persons without significant congregational experience or deep knowledge of the Bible were enrolling at CUTS to prepare for ordained or lay leadership in churches. This shift would call for more basic Bible courses.

Don was heartened when he thought how CUTS's distinctive approach to urban ministry education had shaped its courses, programs, and teaching approaches. The administration's goal was to recruit faculty experienced in urban ministry, with strong knowledge of the subject matter and excellent facilitative skills. CUTS's instructional method sought to combine practical experience in the urban church and classroom instruction that drew on students' experience. CUTS provided in-service workshops to assist faculty with adult learning styles, stressing discussion and active learner involvement to develop students' critical thinking skills. Don reflected, however, that "our teaching methods are both a blessing and a problem. We help many students get high school equivalency who then go on to attain degrees. But all this takes time, individual tutoring, special assistance, and encouragement."

Don was convinced that CUTS's action/reflection model of education had also reaped great benefits for the area churches. He turned over in his mind some of the required B.A. thesis projects students had developed and applied: ministry to those with HIV/AIDS, a mentoring system for congregational youth, a support group ministry for women in abused relationships, after-school tutorial programs, and community analysis and strategy for a new church start. Don nodded to himself as he thought, "Theology is best done in praxis. The church must understand its community context so that it can be an effective agent for justice in the community through a biblically sound, spiritually invigorating, and socially transforming ministry." He chafed over traditional accreditation standards that limited credit for field education and activities outside of a formal classroom.

Don was sure that the experience-based approach and individualized attention to students' needs paid off. He smiled to himself, remembering times when he went to a church, or meeting, or conference, and someone walked up to him and said, "I feel blessed to have gone to CUTS. I received such a solid theological grounding there." "At seminary I was required to read a book that I had already read at CUTS." Former students talked about the relationships with the faculty and the faculty's dedication and commitment. Don thought with satisfaction, "That makes it all worthwhile."

Worrisome Challenges

It was clear that CUTS's teaching methods contrasted sharply with the classical pedagogies generally found in accredited institutions. CUTS's approach was labor intensive and therefore costly in terms of dollars, time, and energy. CUTS staff members prided themselves on their ability to respond to the needs of the urban church. As the needs changed, CUTS changed its courses. Traditional educational institutions did not alter their curriculums frequently or quickly. Thus, CUTS continually defended its course content and the use of adjunct faculty experienced in urban ministry. Such was the case with a newly designed computer science sequence. CUTS students had identified the need, and CUTS staff found faculty with the skills to teach the courses. However, students would not receive academic credit because the courses were not Geneva or Westminster courses, and the process for approval of curricular changes was protracted.

Don thought about some of their staff and part-time faculty who considered real ministry to be evangelism, preaching, and teaching God's Word. They were uneasy about the direction of curriculum changes at CUTS that incorporated preparation for such life/work skills as computer literacy and personnel management. Don felt that other critics romanticized CUTS by saying that it should stay small, maintain close personal relationships, and be a Bible college — when Don knew that it had never been a Bible college.

Some of these same members of staff and faculty were also uncomfortable with gradual changes in the nature of the student body. While the majority of students were still bi-vocational clergy and laity who needed basic academic credentials, an increasing number were more interested in training for secular employment. Don's mental response was, "Our goal is to be responsive to the changing needs of our constituency."

He continued to think about the personnel issues that persistently troubled CUTS. Historically, primary criteria for selecting faculty and staff had been experience and dedication to the students and CUTS's ministry. Over forty predominantly male, part-time adjunct faculty rotated teaching assignments. Some had recognized academic credentials and also taught in other local educational institutions. Many, however, did not possess credentials, such as a Ph.D., that would be recognized by other academic institutions.

Frequently, faculty members recruited both from congregations and from area colleges had been educated in traditional lecturer-recipient models of learning. Although many benefited from CUTS's in-service faculty workshops, others found it difficult to shift their emphasis from delivering content to be learned. Some faculty also resisted developing computer skills to support CUTS's exploration of new educational technologies that used e-mail, the Internet, and technologically based methods of distance learning.

Don was still troubled by the controversy generated by recent faculty terminations. The only three full-time and several part-time faculty members were let go in a downsizing effort. Don knew this had stirred up a lot of strife. Some people said that it was evidence that CUTS would have to close. Others concluded that those terminated weren't in agreement with CUTS's expanded directions. Others perceived racial overtones since two of the faculty were Caucasian. But Don was convinced that the terminations were due solely to financial constraints.

During the spring of 1999, a new academic dean, who taught full-time at a state university, was hired to fill a part-time position with CUTS. Don knew that the dean had been hired because he had a track record as a "turn-around" specialist; he was attracted to CUTS because of its "fantastic mission and committed staff." The new dean immediately began to implement administrative changes such as scheduling courses more than one semester in advance, initiating a formal student recruitment program, outsourcing some computer education modules, and employing faculty from area colleges, businesses, nonprofit organizations, and government agencies who had academic credentials, especially the Ph.D., in addition to practical experience. Then last week, six months after his arrival, the dean announced his resignation in order to return to his former university. His impending departure meant that Don would soon assume the responsibilities for academic oversight in addition to his already demanding administrative load.

Don focused on the financial issues. From the beginning, finding the money to keep CUTS's vision alive had been problematic. CUTS did not have an endowment. It relied on annual donations and, increasingly, on tuition income. This placed additional burdens on students, frequently with families, who often borrowed heavily to finance their education. Paradoxically, CUTS's partnership with Geneva and Westminster inhibited endowment efforts. Formally, these schools awarded the degrees. The CUTS alumni/ae then received the usual contacts and mailings from Westminster and Geneva, not CUTS. Without a strong base of graduate support, pursuit of other sources of academic funding was difficult for CUTS.

Don recalled CUTS's failed attempt to generate endowment intended to help lower students' costs. CUTS and Geneva, along with many other prominent educational and charitable organizations, were involved in the Foundation for New Era Philanthropy fundraising debacle. He vividly recalled reading about the Foundation's collapse. CUTS, having borrowed money to make the investment, would have to shut the doors if it couldn't repay the money. CUTS froze spending, and all staff members took pay cuts. Although CUTS recouped over 90 percent of the initial investment, the remaining debt was still a burden.

CUTS faced other financial challenges with their buildings. In 1983 CUTS had purchased and renovated the house that initially served as both classroom and administrative office space. Now the Archdiocese had decided to sell the academic center CUTS had been leasing for classes since 1991. Even if CUTS could buy the building, it was located several blocks away from the administrative offices. Students complained about their difficulty finding administrators in the evening. In addition, Don had no idea where CUTS would get the money.

Is Accreditation *THE* Answer?

Independent accreditation had been an issue for CUTS almost from the beginning. Don was increasingly convinced that this would be their key to survival and future vitality. With independent accreditation, CUTS could offer degrees that would augment the degree options already available to students through the partnerships with Geneva and Westminster. He was sure that staff could best fulfill God's call to serve urban communities by taking decision-making authority into their own hands.

Don was unsure how to deal with the members of the staff and faculty who maintained that the time, energy, and dollars required to pursue independent accreditation would detract from CUTS's principal call to support urban church leadership. Some maintained that brokering educational partnerships was CUTS's distinctive niche and should be continued. Still others felt that CUTS could accomplish the same goals as independent accreditation by becoming a branch campus of Geneva, an option resisted by Geneva. However, Don had learned that a branch was also subject to a full accreditation review.

Don knew that accreditation placed additional demands on an academic institution. Accrediting teams were concerned about long-term viability and wanted to see a solid financial foundation. Accreditors looked for sufficient resources for facility acquisition and expansion; full-time, fully credentialed faculty; financial aid for students; a library; and additional instructional services. He felt frustrated thinking about the seemingly anachronistic standards. For example, accrediting bodies insisted on full library services. He muttered to himself, "There's so much available on the Internet and through distance learning. Urban pastors are already using these resources. But to be accredited, we need a library. This requirement turns the whole focus away from mission to chasing the dollar to build a library."

Don also questioned the reliance of accrediting bodies on traditionally trained faculty holding doctorates instead of valuing the experience and expertise of effective urban leaders. Another serious question was the accreditation issue of "seat hour" rules that limited credit for activities outside the classroom. In Don's mind this was essentially "You haven't heard it right unless you heard it in a classroom," when all ministry practitioners know better. It was clear from the ministry projects that retention increased dramatically for students who were actively using what they were learning.

Yet Don remained intent on obtaining accreditation as a free-standing, degree-granting institution, even if the additional financial demands would temporarily aggravate their strained budget. He was encouraged by a recent meeting with the Middle States accreditation representative, who clarified the steps to accreditation. Don had already begun revising educational policy and procedure, personnel, and financial manuals. He thought about the strategic plan that emphasized increases in staffing, student retention, enrollment, financial development, and acquisition of classroom facilities. He saw the real problem as convincing all the other players and decision makers that accreditation was THE answer.

Upcoming Meeting

All these issues were on Don's mind as he prepared the agenda for the meeting with the president and the dean, who was still assisting them with future planning. In the five years Don and the president had worked together, Don knew that they shared a common vision and that the president understood the issues facing CUTS. Don felt, however, that the dean did not fully understand the complexity of CUTS — its history, its mission to the city, its many ethnic communities, and the sacrifices people had made for its survival.

"Times are changing," thought Don, "and we have to change with the times. We must plan for it and move ahead — now. This means taking an aggressive path toward accreditation. I keep reminding myself, God has been sufficient to provide in the past. A lot will turn on the outcome of this meeting." Don turned to his cannibalized computer to hammer out the agenda.

Background: Service and Survival
Center for Urban Theological Studies

In the late 1960s and 1970s the social and religious demographics of Philadelphia were rapidly changing. Many predominantly African-American, bi-vocational urban pastors, struggling with the challenges of urban ministry in this setting, were seeking additional training. Most, however, had been apprenticed as church leaders or attended Bible institutes and did not have an undergraduate degree from an accredited college, a requirement for seminary admission. In 1971, Dr. William Krispin, acting on behalf of four African-American urban pastors, asked Westminster Theological Seminary to provide informal seminars on the seminary campus located in a suburb of Philadelphia. In 1973, what was known as the Westminster Saturday Seminar became a more formalized, non-degree, non-accredited diploma program known as the Westminster Ministerial Institute (WMI) under the direction of Dr. Harvie Conn, a Westminster faculty member.

WMI graduates wanted to continue their studies and transfer to the more traditional courses offered at Westminster Theological Seminary. In response, Krispin, successor to Conn as WMI director, sought to develop a college-level program in partnership with an area college. WMI became incorporated in July 1978 as the Center for Urban Theological Studies (CUTS) and began offering accredited courses by September of that year through Geneva College, located in Beaver Falls, Pennsylvania.

CUTS's founders agreed that their primary responsibility was to the local church. "We didn't take an agenda from a school and force it upon the ministries in a community. Instead, we strove to echo the voice and sentiments of the local church. As a result, we maintained a certain amount of autonomy from our sponsoring schools that we have not found in other programs."[1] The founders also defined ministerial edu-

---

1. Quoted passages come from official publications of the seminary or from interviews with seminary personnel.

91

cation in terms other than the prevailing paradigm of master's-level training. CUTS programs became an extension of the next level of training given in Bible institutes or in on-the-job apprenticeship models for church leaders who did not have an undergraduate education.

Acknowledging that there were many constituencies in the city that might be served, CUTS declared unswerving commitment to a specific constituency. This original commitment continues to shape its mission. The statement of purpose in the preamble to CUTS's constitution highlights the importance of the empowerment of that constituency as well as the importance of bridges of reconciliation in order to share resources with other communities.

> Article 11. We confess with shame the sinful division within the body of Christ that has been caused by racial and cultural prejudice. Early in our nation's history, the church was divided into alienated units when white Christians failed to receive their black brothers and sisters into the fullness of fellowship and ministry in the church. This sinful schism in the United States was the result of the white people stealing black people from their African home and cruelly enslaving them to the destruction of family and personal integrity. This alienation continues today and manifests itself in our failure both to submit and to minister to one another. Alienation can also be seen in other ethnic and poor church communities in the United States. The unity of the body of Christ necessitates that these churches today actively seek ways of meeting each other's needs.

Furthermore, the continuing racism, classism, individual sin and corporate structural evils in our society have had a devastating effect on major portions of the urban population. Hardest hit have been African Americans and educationally disenfranchised ethnic groups. Thus, the opportunities for higher education have either been altogether denied to them or have been effectively nullified by inadequate educational preparation and provision. The urban church that has arisen in this situation has developed a non-formal model of ministerial training, in contrast to the pattern of formal academic preparation in colleges and graduate schools of theology.

The non-formal model of training characteristic of urban ethnic churches has strengths that formal academic education lacks. The strengths of this apprenticeship model include the development of maturity, the practical demonstration and improvement of ministerial gifts, and the establishment of fellowship between the leader and the church served. Further, the oral communication that preserved the gospel in the black church nurtured genuine depth of understanding.

If the cycle of racism, classism, and non-recognition of the competence of these church leaders is to be broken, a fair assessment of true competence must be developed. Also, credentialed theological training must be made attainable for these church leaders within the apprenticeship model of their churches as well as Christian educational institutions.

Further, churches among African Americans and disenfranchised ethnic groups and the rest of Christ's church must begin to heal the racial and cultural divisions by seeking to strengthen one another and to open avenues for communication and sharing of resources.

These needs find their meaning and urgency in the unity of Christ's church and her calling to preach good news to the poor, proclaim freedom for the prisoners, recovery of sight for the blind, liberation for the oppressed, and to announce that the time has come when the Lord will save His people. The full ministry of the church in word and deed must be a leaven in society and a light to the world. Thus, it is to these needs that the purpose of the Center for Urban Theological Studies is addressed.

At the time of the case study, the late 1990s, CUTS mission continued to provide education, training, and resources to develop servant-leaders for the urban church, community, and marketplace. CUTS offered the following programs in order to fulfill this mission:

- Accredited undergraduate education in partnership with Geneva College, Beaver Falls, Pennsylvania
- Accredited graduate education in partnership with Westminster Theological Seminary, Chestnut Hill (Glenside), Pennsylvania
- Consulting services in areas such as urban church planting and urban church resources

"How to make a person better in ministry and how to make a person more efficient in whatever ministry God has called them to" frames the way CUTS's staff views programmatic changes. At no point has CUTS seen itself solely as a "school." CUTS's staff and administrators continue to be involved in consulting and programmatic support — helping people, churches, and denominations enhance the ministry of the urban church.

Discussion Notes: Service and Survival

Teaching Goals on Community and Curriculum

- To explore principles for determining how curriculum is shaped.
- To identify bridges and barriers to survival for non-traditional institutions such as CUTS.
- To explore elements of strategic, long-range planning for non-traditional, urban theological institutions.

Note: The authors suggest that, because of its length and complexity, this case should be distributed to discussion participants and read prior to the time set for discussion.

I. Mission and Curriculum

A. Identify changes in CUTS's student population since its beginning in 1978. (Note, for example, the shift from 90 percent pastors to 33 percent pastors and 66 percent laity.) How have these changes affected curriculum decisions?

B. Identify CUTS's primary program partners and clarify their relationship as presented in the case. What roles have these partners played in determining curriculum?

C. What are CUTS's criteria for determining curriculum to accomplish its mission to prepare a predominantly urban, African-American, church-related constituency for quality employment and effective servant ministry to the church and community?

In light of the previous discussion, consider what parameters should guide a theological educational institution in making curricular decisions. What theological presuppositions should inform these decisions?

II. Building Communities to Sustain Non-Traditional Educational Institutions

A. Identify CUTS's primary assets for and the most reliable bridges to long-term sustainability. (Consider CUTS's history, its innovative role as an educational broker, student and church support, and so forth.)

B. What are the primary liabilities and barriers to CUTS's long-term sustainability?

C. Divide the discussion group into three sections. Assign each small group the following identities:

1. Staff and faculty, like Donald Gardner, who support independent accreditation as the most viable route to CUTS's survival.

2. Staff and faculty opposed to independent accreditation.

3. CUTS students asked for your reflections about the future of CUTS.

Allow 10-15 minutes for each group to discuss and build its position. Call for a selected representative to present a brief statement for each group before entering a facilitated plenary discussion among the three groups. Allow a minimum of 15 minutes for this discussion.

D. In light of the discussions about CUTS's mission, history, and approach to the future, have the full group offer their own suggestions for sustaining CUTS's program, supporting these suggestions with their own theological and organizational rationale.

III. Additional Questions and Concerns for Clergy and Church Lay Leaders

Many urban congregations are struggling with their identity, constituency, and mission in light of often dramatic social and economic changes. Church programming can be analogous to the curriculum of an institution such as CUTS. Use a discussion of this case to help congregational leaders discuss what is foundational to their mission and which elements are changeable in order to develop more effective ministries.

Case Study: A Shifting of Paradigms

"I've looked through the course listing for the Fall Semester, and all I see is courses that fulfill degree requirements," complained Rev. Joseph Whittaker. "What happened to the courses that were offered for those in the Diploma Program or for the beginning student who wants to take only one course for a certificate of completion? You used to have a much broader selection of courses. I was really looking for something that would help me train new members of my church's Board of Deacons."

Jean Farmer, Assistant Director of Student Advisement for the Center for Urban Ministerial Education, sighed. "We don't offer a course like that this year. I will bring that idea to the curriculum committee. In the meantime, perhaps you could take one of the New Testament courses which requires the use of Greek and see if the professor would allow you to take the course utilizing only English. This is less than ideal, but it would allow you to take the one New Testament course you need to complete the ten-course Diploma. Let me make a couple of calls, and I'll get back to you."

Rev. Whittaker nodded his assent as he rose from the chair. "Okay, I'll wait to hear from you," he said to Farmer and to Edward Samson, CUME's associate director, who had been in on the conversation. After the local pastor left, Jean turned to Ed. "He's right, of course.

This case was written by Bruce W. Jackson. The names of all persons in this case are disguised to protect the privacy of those involved in the situation.

Our curriculum is more rigid than before. I wonder if it's still serving CUME's target communities. We really do need to discuss this at our staff meeting this afternoon." Just then Jean's phone rang. As she took the call, Ed excused himself and returned to his office.

With Whittaker's visit fresh in his mind, Ed picked up the memorandum he had read dozens of times. The words still stung even after the distance of two years: "You have failed to comprehend the true nature of the subject under discussion." The memo referred to events leading to the opening of a programmatic site at Boston's historic Park Street Church. Even though the heat of that moment had passed, Ed wondered aloud, "I know that this memo refers to a particular event, but it continues to reflect the crux of the matter. Does any of us really grasp what seems to be happening here at CUME? Aren't we really arguing about our very soul?" Samson replaced the memo in the file and leaned back in his chair. He tried to recall the events that led to this turning point in CUME's history.

The Center for Urban Ministerial Education was founded in 1976 in response to a clearly identified need for theological education specifically contextualized to the inner city — "a theological educational program socio-culturally relevant to the promises and challenges of urban reality." CUME's Founding Director was convinced that many of the most gifted people in urban ministry did not have access to the traditional route to seminary education. In his words, "It's not that people don't want an education, but due to social, economic, or personal reasons, they have been unable to fulfill the prerequisites for higher education. In effect, they are locked out of the very system that could enhance their ministry effectiveness and closed off from the wider society that demands recognized credentials." The founding director established CUME to bring the resources of a major seminary into contact with the neighborhoods where practicing ministers and church leaders were located — the heart of the urban church.

Even before official approval that a degree could be granted, CUME's courses were geared to a master's level. A student's previous ministry experience was valued and validated. The ten-course Diploma Program was designed to demonstrate that a student could satisfactorily fulfill the requirements for entrance into a degree program. However, students and faculty saw the diploma as a valued credential in its own right, serving as the terminating point for a large number of students. Many students said that the Diploma Program was "a great source of strength" for their congregations.

Qualified students who combined significant ministry experience, completed the Diploma, and made a formal application were eligible for entrance into a master's degree program. This structure meant that persons who lacked the baccalaureate degree, but who had significant urban ministry experience, could still have access to solid theological education. Those who had the traditional education prerequisites could enter directly into a degree program if they were accepted through the traditional application procedures.

CUME's sponsoring seminary was located some thirty-five miles north of Boston in a suburban community. The South Hamilton campus of Gordon-Conwell emphasized a classical theological education, with particular strengths in Bible and theology. While the CUME program retained the strong emphases in Bible and theology, most courses originally focused on a "contextualized approach." CUME also emphasized serving those who had been most marginalized from theological education — theologically and socially stated: "the poor." From the start, CUME offered classes in English and Spanish. Since 1982, two additional language tracks, French (for Haitians) and Portuguese (for Brazilians, Portuguese, Cape Verdean, and the Azores), were added to serve CUME's multiethnic, multilingual constituencies. From 1990 through 1995 CUME offered Theological Education for the Deaf. Classes ranging from five to seven students were taught entirely in American Sign Language.

Ed Samson and other staff members agreed that for a large portion of CUME's beginning years, the distance between the two campuses was not a hindrance. CUME enjoyed a wide degree of freedom with regard to curriculum design, engaging adjunct professors, and policy decisions. Relations between CUME's founding director and the dean of the seminary were cordial and marked by mutual trust, which allowed unprecedented freedom for CUME to tailor courses to respond to issues and events in the inner city. CUME experienced steady and significant growth in terms of student enrollments, number of courses offered, and the complexity of its programs. Ed realized, however, that with growth in any new program, the inevitable institutionalization process begins to exert its impact.

As Ed reflected about the purposes that guided CUME since its founding, he ticked off events that seemed to have contributed to the present turning point. There was the push to establish the Master of Divinity at CUME. As early as 1987 an evaluation and long-range planning project documented that the students, staff, and administrators from both the South Hamilton campus and CUME saw the M.Div. as the next logical step in CUME's development. Qualified students who lacked an undergraduate degree could enter through the ten-course Diploma, earn the twenty-course M.A. degree, and then go on to complete the M.Div. degree.

A task force composed of CUME representatives, Gordon-Conwell faculty, and Gordon-Conwell administrators was established. In record time, less than a year, the degree was planned. CUME staff had not questioned the assumption that the degree would generally follow the outline of courses taught at Gordon-Conwell, including the strong emphasis on biblical languages, theology, and practical ministry courses. Ed recalled with a wry smile that several South Hamilton faculty members had rather naïvely asked if persons of color were able to master the biblical languages! Though the outline of the degree followed traditional patterns, it was understood that the M.Div. would be contextualized to the urban setting, similar to the Diploma and M.A. degree. The composition of the faculty, the language of instruction, the location and time of the courses, and, of course, the ethos that the students, as adult learners, brought to the class all reflected CUME's contextualized approach. It was also assumed that CUME's historical emphasis on providing in-service theological education for people who found themselves excluded from the traditional avenues of access would be maintained. The announcement at the 1989 CUME banquet that the M.Div. was approved by the faculty and trustees was met with overwhelming acclaim by those present. The community clearly welcomed access to the new degree.

Expansion of the academic program led to the matter of a CUME administrative building. In 1990, after almost eight years of pushing for a building, the staff relocated to its present site, excited about finally having adequate space. The move from the original, rented location in the Roxbury section of Boston — one of the more impoverished areas of the city — to the Jamaica Plain section — a mixed but mostly poor neighborhood — was made after careful deliberations as to what messages, implicit and explicit, might be sent. Issues of visibility, identity, access to mass transit, parking, and the perceptions of neighborhood safety were all factors that contributed to the decision. Still, CUME staff were convinced that the symbol of a permanent site, owned by the seminary, would send a powerful message to the community that Gordon-Conwell was indeed serious about maintaining an urban presence beyond the level of tokenism.

With pride, students referred to the building located on South Huntington Avenue in the Jamaica Plain section of Boston as *"our building."* However, Ed recalled that one of CUME's noted visiting professors made a telling comment: "You know, now that you have the M.Div. on line and have acquired a building, you are moving into a more institutionalized existence. The 'powers-that-be' will be paying a whole lot more attention to you now. The relative autonomy that you initially experienced may be a thing of the past."

"Maybe that's it," thought Ed. "Maybe what we are experiencing is simply the result of growing pains in the institutionalization process." Still, his uneasiness led him to open the file on his desk and reread the series of memoranda that had been sent back and forth during the 1992-93 academic year when he served as CUME's acting director. Initially, that year was supposed to be one in which CUME would be officially recognized as a branch campus. When that decision was postponed until the following academic year, Ed recalled feeling ambivalent. He rationalized that postponement would make his job less stressful. He could concentrate on maintaining the program, expecting that the campus development would move ahead upon the director's return from administrative leave.

"The best laid plans of mice and men," he mused aloud. The caretaker role Ed expected for the academic year was thrown on end with an announcement from the seminary administration that Gordon-Conwell's urban program would be expanded to include a program at the historic Park Street Church, located in the heart of the business district in downtown Boston. The church was noted for its active mission program, ministry with international students, and a growing presence in ministry to the marketplace, particularly with its young adult group. The church drew most of its congregation from suburban communities and included people who were of some influence in the city's business, government, and professional sectors. Park Street Church had recently acquired two buildings adjacent to its sanctuary and planned an extensive renovation and expansion into the new space. Congregational leaders expressed a desire "to reconnect to the city."

Looking back on the announcement, Ed realized this was the first indication that there was a difference in how some at the seminary interpreted ministry in the city. Ed picked up a second memo from September 1992 that seemed to confirm his impression. He read: "A process [will be initiated] that will lead to a set of proposals involving programs and teaching staff at CUME in both the diploma and degree tracks with a view toward efficiency and effectiveness . . . and the viability of urban-based programs in partnership with Park Street Church on the basis of a redefinition of the urban education concept and the forecast of new student markets among international students and marketplace workers." At the time this was received, Ed recalled that his conversations with the new seminary dean had centered on fiscal concerns. Strong statements were made that CUME was becoming a "drag" on the overall seminary budget because it was not self-sustaining. Later it would be stated that the redefinition and expansion of the urban programs to the Park Street site and the anticipated revenue they produced would be, in the dean's words, "CUME's salvation."

Ed caught himself thinking, "Isn't it ironic that the message sent to CUME was: 'You need to be self-supporting.' Yet no one ever asks if classes offered in Ugaritic are self-supporting." He even recalled a high-level administrator's comment that CUME needed to focus more on the bottom line and not be so "mission driven."

With a sigh, Ed recalled the tension in fall of 1992 over the establishment of the site at Park Street. It wasn't so much that CUME opposed the seminary administration's wanting to expand its presence in Boston, nor was it against Park Street Church looking for creative ways to become more closely connected to its urban location. CUME had always encouraged the widest participation of people from all over the city. In fact, the CUME student body represented the breadth and scope of the metropolitan area and included students from as far south as Rhode Island and Connecticut, as far north as Maine, and from western Massachusetts. CUME's founding director had always insisted that the entire city was CUME's "parish."

The clash seemed to center around the basic, underlying educational philosophy that would drive the curriculum, specifically which community was going to serve as the overall focal point for CUME's future development. CUME staff argued that the organizing principle should be one of serving students who were based in the neighborhoods. CUME's founding director had often reminded the staff of the dictum, "You get to the universal through the particular." He used Jesus' incarnation in the plan of redemption as an illustration. By this he meant that if you focus on the people most in need of urban theological education, in his words "the poor," those who had access to greater resources would also find a way to utilize the program.

The dean of the seminary, however, insisted that Gordon-Conwell's urban thrust should reflect a "metropolitan" viewpoint as opposed to the inner city. He argued that an expanded vision of "urban" should include the marketplace and international students. The dean cited an interest by business and professional people in taking educational offerings that would help strengthen their Christian witness in their occupations. He argued that Park Street Church's large ministry to international students made it a natural location to attract this new constituency. In fact, several seminary trustees and the pastor of Park Street Church were quite enthusiastic about the partnership of offering classes at the church. They felt that the marketplace focus would be appreciated and well received.

During subsequent conversations with the dean, Ed made the observation that several CUME students who were business people and entrepreneurs were based in the neighborhoods, not downtown. He saw possibilities for new avenues of dialogue between the neighborhoods and the business district that would be in line with CUME's historic thrust to provide access to marginalized populations. A partnership would be an opportunity for two distinct population centers to meet. Ed had suggested, "Perhaps classes could be held at both locations — facilitating relationships between downtown and the neighborhoods in a way that the secular community could not." However, the dean proposed changing the structure of the entire Boston campus administration, relocating the administrative offices to Park Street, selling the administrative building in Jamaica Plain, and making CUME one of several programmatic thrusts of the seminary's urban offerings.

The CUME staff raised questions about the educational philosophy being expounded. Was it really a matter of redefining urban ministry? If so, what lay behind it? Was location in an inner-city neighborhood really the issue? Did people think that CUME's teaching sites were unsafe at night? Ironically, Ed recalled a black student from Roxbury telling him that she felt unsafe attending classes on Park Street because it was a "dangerous area" at night. Yet several whites had intimated the same reluctance about going to Roxbury or Boston's South End neighborhoods for the same reason. In fact, one of his students came to Ed after the new programs at the Park Street site were announced and asked bluntly, "Is this development at Park Street kind of a CUME for the white folks — for those who don't want to come into the neighborhoods?" A hard question, but one that deserved an answer. At the time, Ed knew the CUME staff members had similar questions but didn't voice them aloud.

Ed felt that a distinguished theological educator had capsulized the matter well when he stated, "Historically, what CUME has been about is bringing the resources of a major seminary to serve those most underserved by theological education. It represents a powerful statement of the center moving to serve at the margins, instead of asking those at the margins to come into the center." Would the redefinition of urban ministry referred to by the seminary dean result in reorienting the focus on the center at the expense of the margins? It seemed to Ed that the paradigm was shifting. He kept asking, "Is this what we really want? Is this what Scripture demands? Is this what the Lord wants?"

"Staff meeting. Five minutes to staff meeting," crackled the voice of CUME's office manager over the intercom. Ed snapped out of his reverie. "Be right there," he said. Ed sighed deeply as he gathered his papers and files for the staff meeting. Curricular matters would dominate the agenda, and he knew it was going to be a long meeting. He recalled the office manager's observations from last week's staff meeting: "I think we are offering far too many courses for the degree programs. We're neglecting our Diploma students, who are the heart of CUME! Students who want to take just one course are frustrated because we mostly offer courses that meet degree requirements. We should be offering more issue-oriented courses, more courses of a timely, topical nature." Her observations seemed right on target, especially in light of the meeting he and Jean had this morning with Rev. Whittaker. Since the opening of the site at Park Street, the curriculum did seem to slant more heavily toward fulfilling degree requirements. "But we *have* to offer courses that meet requirements in order for degree students to make progress in their programs," mumbled Ed aloud.

Ed reflected further on last week's meeting. The issue of the number of courses to be offered in the various language tracks surfaced, but was tabled for today's meeting. What could be done to increase the number of courses in Spanish, French, and Portuguese? CUME has already closed the Theological Education for the Deaf (American Sign Language) program because the seminary administration had determined that the population of deaf students was too small to justify its cost. Ed also knew CUME was now offering only half as many courses in Spanish as ten years ago. A staff member had sardonically observed, "We could attract more students in our language tracks if we could offer more courses, while the seminary is telling us that we must have more students in order to justify offering more courses."

"There's still the matter of how the seminary can continue to sponsor essentially two distinct urban programs," thought Ed as he searched for his datebook and a pen. "We have CUME and the Park Street site, each in the same city, yet focusing on different populations. When we realized that CUME staff was providing operational support for both urban sites with no accrual of the tuition from the Park Street courses to our budget, we declined to continue administering the design and delivery of courses taught there. Logistically, that presents us now with the problem of offering courses that compete with one another — a situation that has already occurred."

"Something's got to change," thought Ed as he entered the conference room and took his seat.

Background: A Shifting of Paradigms
Center for Urban Ministerial Education

Gordon-Conwell Theological Seminary's commitment to the urban scene is rooted in the rich heritage of the two schools that merged in 1969, forming one evangelical institution. At the time of the merger, The Conwell School of Theology, founded in 1884 by Russell Conwell, had a distinctive emphasis on educating urban clergy. Likewise, Gordon Divinity School, founded in 1889 by A. J. Gordon, shared a historical concern for missions in New England's urban centers and abroad.

After a series of efforts to honor the merger's intent to provide a theological education program for the city, the Urban Year Program was launched in 1973. Then known as the "Urban Middler Year," it offered residential seminary students an "urban year" of living, ministering, and studying in the inner-city and working-class sections of metropolitan Boston. Eldin Villafañe, a Puerto Rican Pentecostal pastor studying for his Ph.D. in Social Ethics at Boston University, was hired in July 1976 to direct the fledgling urban program and to offer "a few classes" for urban pastors and church leaders. Concentrating his efforts on the second task, he launched the Center for Urban Ministerial Education (CUME) in September 1976 to serve the adult, multiethnic, urban constituency. Villafañe had long noted an urgent need for training specifically designed for urban church leaders already in ministry. While such leaders were quite capable of serious theological study, social, economic, and educational realities often locked them out of traditional routes to quality theological education. The Urban Year program was originally administered separately from CUME, but in 1985 the two merged to create a unified approach to urban ministry training.

Meeting at the Martin Luther King, Jr. House of the historic Twelfth Baptist Church, with an initial enrollment of 30 students, CUME grew numerically and programmatically. Initially, the curriculum for urban leaders consisted of two programs: The Certificate Program, an "incentive building mechanism"; and the Diploma of Religious Education. The Diploma was a ten-course program with a

107

prescribed curriculum of six required courses and four electives. Courses were offered on a credit basis with the hope and expectation that all courses would eventually be accepted as part of a degree that was yet to be named. Some courses in the Diploma program were soon offered in five languages.

In 1980, Gordon-Conwell Seminary approved CUME's offering of the Master of Religious Education (M.R.E.) degree in two distinct tracks. Students with a college degree could apply directly for admission into the degree program. Those who lacked an undergraduate degree, but who had completed the ten-course CUME Diploma, were 35 years or older, had seven years of ministry experience (five if the student had successfully completed a Bible institute program), and completed the formal application process, could enter the M.R.E. degree program. Courses for this degree could be taken entirely in Spanish, making CUME one of the few U.S. theological institutions where this was possible for a master's-level degree. The opening up of a master's degree track for students who did not possess a college degree, but who had significant ministry experience, was a major factor in fueling CUME's growth for the next decade. With the arrival of the M.R.E. degree and the first graduates in 1982, student enrollments climbed rapidly, typically reaching close to 200 students per semester for the next few years. Anglo, African-American, Haitian, Hispanic, and Portuguese-speaking students were proportionally representative of the area population. In October 1990 CUME moved from rented space to ownership of a building in the Jamaica Plain section of Boston.

As the number of M.R.E. and Diploma graduates grew, there was increased clamor for the addition of the Master of Divinity (M.Div.) degree. In response to this demand, the M.Div. in Urban Ministries was designed during the 1988 academic year and launched in 1989. As part of the M.Div. degree, and later the M.A. in Urban Ministries, the Mentored Ministry program was developed to meet supervised ministry requirements, stipulated by ATS standards. Unique in its approach, Mentored Ministry paired CUME students with experienced peer mentors for regular meetings of theological reflection. Course work in the form of several colloquia provided for theological input. Peer groups, led by trained student leaders, emerged to encourage the action-reflection model. Mentored Ministry serves as an integrating factor in the overall CUME curriculum.

In 1992 CUME moved into a period of transition as student enrollments began an overall decline. These were first disguised and offset by combining student enrollment figures with those of a new teaching site at the Park Street Church in Boston. At the time of the case, analysis by CUME staff indicated that changes in policies and course emphases, combined with a changing church situation, contributed to the decline in numbers. With the increased emphasis on the degree programs by both the seminary and CUME and the concomitant need to offer courses that met degree requirements, the curriculum appeared to be less attractive to Diploma Program students who did not aspire to a degree but rather saw the Diploma as their terminal credential. During this same period, the Certificate Program was dropped from the curriculum.

Gordon-Conwell Seminary administrators were also exerting pressure on the structure of the programs and the selection of faculty at CUME. Where once CUME had autonomy in the selection of teachers based upon their experience and commitment to urban ministry as well as their academic credentials — in some cases pairing an experienced ministry practitioner with a more academically credentialed person to "team teach" a course — the seminary increasingly emphasized academic credentials. In some cases faculty proposed by CUME administrators were not accepted by the parent institution on the basis of ecclesiological or theological differences. A concern to comply with the admission standards of the Association of Theological Schools (ATS) was cited as one reason for such increased control by the seminary. The seminary also cited financial pressures brought on by decreasing tuition revenue; increased costs, including maintenance of the CUME site; and the Foundation for New Era Philanthropy collapse as reasons for budget cutbacks.

At the time of the case, questions remained as to whether the original philosophy of education would continue to guide CUME's future or whether a different paradigm of urban ministry — one focused upon a redefinition of "urban" with a concomitant differing ecclesiological emphasis — would cause CUME's historic mission and emphasis to continue to shift from a non-traditional urban theological education program to a more traditional academic theological education program.

Discussion Notes: A Shifting of Paradigms

Teaching Goals on Community and Curriculum

- To consider the meaning of "urban" and, consequently, the goals of urban ministry.
- To explore the factors that shape and determine the development of curriculum.
- To explore approaches for urban ministry centers to relate constructively to academic host institutions.
- To develop guidelines for congregations and organizations to address conflicts fueled by tension between "mission-driven" and "survival-determined" programs.

I. Opening Exercise

Ask the group to self-identify those who grew up or currently live in the city and those who were raised and live in a suburban or rural area.

Pass out sheets of blank paper. Ask discussion participants to draw their most immediate image of "the city." Invite people to share their drawing and explain the symbolism.

Ask the group about differences between those images drawn by people who were raised or live in the city and those who were socialized in suburban or rural areas.

Ask what implications the different "views" of the city have for urban ministry.

II. Questions for Discussion

1. CUME is part of two communities: its academic home, which resides in the suburbs, and its ministry, which resides in the city. What different understandings of "urban" emerge from the case study? What factors have shaped these images? What perspectives might influence the choice between using the term "metropolitan" or "inner city" to describe the urban context?

2. How do socialized patterns or stereotypes of power, success, racism, and classism affect one's view of the city, the concept of who is to be served, and what curriculum components should have priority?

3. Some biblical scholars and pastors see "the preferential option for the poor" [based on numerous scriptures including Jesus' proclamation of "the acceptable year of the Lord" (Luke 4:18-19)] as a biblical imperative. How does this mandate affect one's understanding of the primary constituency for urban ministry?

4. Ask participants to write down what they consider the two most important components of a program to prepare persons for urban ministry. Invite people to share these components and explain why they are essential for effective and faithful urban ministry. Press participants to identify the ministerial paradigm that informs their image of the content, design, or delivery of urban ministry programs.

5. The seminary administration and faculty, the staff of CUME, and CUME students and their congregations are all seeking a role in determining course offerings. What factors should determine which voices have the most influence? Press participants to clarify the assumptions that lie behind their suggestions.

6. Some voices in the case would describe CUME as a branch campus of the seminary. Others see CUME as a center for ministry and service to the city. What are the implications of being seen primarily as a branch or a center? Should degree programs of the

seminary or the CUME certificate and Diploma programs take priority? Ask participants what rationale informs their responses.

7. There is often tension between those advocating mission and those stressing survival. What theological, biblical, and practical factors would press an urban ministry education program toward being "mission-driven" or being "survival-determined," that is, more influenced by the bottom line? Encourage debate and dialogue among discussion participants.

III. Discerning Alternatives

Ask participants to enter the role of an advisor for Ed Samson and other members of the CUME staff.

1. What strategies do you suggest to clarify the issues and build consensus around a common understanding of "urban"?

2. Different communities want the authority to shape the theology, educational philosophy, and priorities for CUME's programs. What steps are most important for getting these communities into constructive dialogue with one another? (Consider elements of power, trust, communication, and transparency.)

3. What advice would you offer seminaries and congregations to deal with the tension between mission and survival? Identify effective ways to keep potentially competing paradigms in creative tension. Consider specific guidelines for an approach that helps parties identify their differences and common concerns, and develop programs that meet the needs of several constituencies.

Commentary

LEAH GASKIN FITCHUE

The subject of Community is at the core of the Center for Urban Theological Studies (CUTS) and the Center for Urban Ministerial Education (CUME). Both began in the middle to late seventies with a vision to serve urban clergy denied theological education opportunities primarily due to the lack of an undergraduate degree. Both began in urban communities occupied primarily by marginalized and poor persons. Both sought to serve as an advocate for urban community empowerment. Both welcomed the opportunity to push the theological envelope in challenging traditionally held access codes that defined church community leadership in ways that included some and excluded others. Both stood boldly before the throne of creativity and sought to craft a path for the self-empowerment of pastors. These were persons who knew how to be church leaders and use the biblical text to preach the gospel, but who did not know how to align their pastoral gifts with the resources of their congregations and communities, in order to serve an increasingly complex, challenging, convoluted urban way of being, living, and dying. Both, as innovators of new theological education blueprints, were called to be tested.

Community

In considering the relationship between an urban ministry program and the community, we are charged to look both within the institution and outside of the institution. Internally, there is culture that unites board members, administrators, staff, faculty, and students in reciprocal relationships. Included in the dynamics of the internal community ethos are multiple interactive factors — physical, mental, and spiritual. Central to the essence and quality of this internal community is the role of its leadership in modeling behavior, which, if it is wise, fosters community inclusiveness, wholeness, stability, and respect. If wisdom is lacking, pseudo community emerges and issues of exclusion, fragmentation, instability, and disrespect prevail.

Community, therefore, for the urban ministry program is always in process of becoming. It balances changing external context and competing internal needs against a background of community compassion or contempt, depending upon the issue, traditions, time, and players. Most program participants come in search of an internal learning community that affirms and validates the quintessence of the external communities from which they come and to which they will return. It is wise leadership, therefore, that serves as a bridge between the internal community and the external community.

Internally or externally, community for the urban ministry program must be viewed holistically, contextually, and paradoxically. Holistically in that no aspect of the urban ministry program is separated from some aspect of community; contextually in that the day-to-day lived experience of community and the program shape the core learning paradigm; paradoxically in that what the urban ministry program may define as its mission may differ from what the community sees as its role or its function. The urban ministry program, as a feeder to and recipient of community, offers a unique opportunity for partnership. The quality of the relationship is ultimately determined by the risks each partner takes and endures in its own transformation. Without this relationship there will be no renewal. Without risks there will be no real community.

The Center for Urban Theological Studies (CUTS)

The pastors who came to CUTS in 1978 were already in their pulpits, many shepherding their congregations full time while working full time in secular employment. CUTS was born, therefore, to assist already established pastors to meet the unique challenges and needs of ministry in a rapidly changing urban milieu. The term "consultant" suited the intent of CUTS to serve as an educational broker in providing clergy training to pastors. CUTS grew out of the Westminster Ministerial Institute (WMI), seeing itself as a unique training resource to enhance ministerial effectiveness for the black church community and trained African-American urban pastors who were "disenfranchised by the predominantly white schools in the area."

CUTS experienced early in its development the tension between being and becoming as it sought to serve its internal community while attempting to be a resource for its external community. In pioneering undergraduate and master's-level ministry training in the evening, CUTS opened up a new world of possibilities for its marginalized students. The impact of this shift, which would permanently alter the ministerial training vision out of which CUTS emerged, appeared to have not been fully grasped or appreciated by the leadership of CUTS. Not only did the pastors want better theological education to transcend their "second-rate stigmas," but they also wanted educational content to help them advance in their secular jobs. The pastors wanted holistic education in order to serve their own cry for human wholeness and that of those whom they shepherded in their various contexts.

While it struggled with calling itself an educational institution, it increasingly served a broader market that demanded access to higher education for both ministerial and secular employment. An interesting, and inevitable, tension emerged with CUTS's shift to accommodate both ministerial training and the secular employment needs of its Christian adult learners. The learning paradigm shifted from linear to holistic, from pastor to lay, from male to female, from church driven to community driven. In the midst of this transition, the question of identity re-emerged. How would CUTS take its agenda from the voice and sentiments of the local church and allow it to be the centerpiece that would drive, shape, and validate each student's learned and lived experience in community? Today, urban ministry programs around the country are struggling with how to align their vision and resource capacities with those they serve and thus maintain their servanthood integrity and independence.

Center for Urban Ministerial Education (CUME)

The tension of expansion that gripped CUME had an enormous impact on its internal and external community. It was in the midst of this transition that CUME learned to struggle with its trinitarian responsibility for community: its internal community, its parental community

(Gordon-Conwell Theological Seminary), and its external community. After it had effectively provided a Master of Arts program during the first decade of its existence, including Master of Divinity studies seemed the next logical step for CUME in advancing theological education for its students. Thus, in 1987 CUME joined with members of Gordon-Conwell Theological Seminary, its parent body, to build a visible path for qualified urban ministers to move through CUME's ten-course Diploma program, and specified M.A. degree courses, in order to be eligible for M.Div. studies. The approval of the M.Div. degree course of study would forever change the life of CUME. It was, unfortunately, a change that was not anticipated and in some instances not appreciated. The inclusion of M.Div. degree studies introduced qualification issues about CUME students that heretofore had not been challenged by Gordon-Conwell Theological Seminary. Some Gordon-Conwell faculty viewed the credentialing of persons who had not traveled the traditional undergraduate degree route for the M.Div. degree as a lessening of academic standards. That these newcomers were for the most part marginalized persons of color made the issue more volatile. In time, CUME's new M.Div. degree would usher in new standards, new demands, new ways of operating, new ways of serving, and new challenges to surviving.

As the tension between CUME and Gordon-Conwell Theological Seminary increased, CUME's assumption about the stability of its contextualized approach for teaching urban ministry was challenged. What had been sacred began to feel violated. What had been urban theological education for the marginalized urban minister of color now became urban theological education for the white downtown marketplace worker. Depending upon its parent body for its financial existence, CUME entered into a parental-offspring conflictual relationship that made CUME examine the very foundation of its identity as it asked the question: What is the mission of CUME, and whose right is it to determine the answer to the question?

Community Learning Principles

The nature of CUTS's and CUME's program partners made an irrevocable imprint on the way in which each came into being, contextualized its identity, learned how to handle its own conflict and survival, and served as a "living witness" for its constituents in the midst of its own transformation. CUTS's brokerage badge led it to seek partners who acknowledged its vision to assist the disenfranchised in their own empowerment. The CUTS partnership with Geneva College and Westminster Theological Seminary was, however, never truly equal, although this is a claim that CUTS embraces tenaciously. While praiseworthy, and at times extraordinary, commitments came from both of these partners to help CUTS transition from dream to its various states of reality, both partners viewed CUTS as an appendage — something to be connected to at a distance. Neither appeared ready to risk its own transformation in the interest of the partnership, and each always realized and protected its power status. For example, Geneva College refused to accept CUTS as a satellite site for fear of injury to its accreditation process; after twenty years of partnering with Westminster Theological Seminary, faculty members maintained a paternalistic view of CUTS as a totally dependent recipient of Westminster's benevolence. Each institution had something that CUTS needed; CUTS had very little that either of these institutions needed or could not acquire through some other source. For CUTS, the partnership was its lifeline; for the partners, CUTS was their community outreach program.

The question for CUTS and other urban ministry programs to consider in shaping its future and strengthening its partnerships is the matter of equality. When partners like Geneva College and Westminster Theological Seminary are larger and more financially solvent, can an equal partnership exist? If an equal partnership is necessary, how is it achieved when issues of power, money, and degree-awarding status are solely controlled by one partner and solely needed by the other? If the proposed biblical model, "I need you and you need me," is at the center of the partnership, how does the partnership honor the distinctives of each member in a way that each is valued, and violation of one member of the partnership reduces the effectiveness of the other?

The CUME concept of partner in ministry to describe the CUME relationship with its parent body is complicated. As CUME developed and expanded, certain basic assumptions were made about the role and existence of CUME that apparently were never clarified by all key participants. CUME assumed, but did not clarify with Gordon-Conwell

Theological Seminary, that its historical emphasis on the marginalized would be maintained, and that every fiber of the degree-granting process would reflect its contextualized urban ministry approach, while honoring the seminary's standards.

As student enrollment declined and new students preferred degree programs, CUME's "drag" on the overall seminary budget weakened its autonomy and apparently led to a parent body directive to shift from non-traditional to more traditional theological education. The dominant tension between CUME and Gordon-Conwell Theological Seminary dealt with the bottom line, and the shift in focus from mission driven to bottom-line driven shook CUME's contextualized urban ministry foundation. What and who would determine the direction of CUME? What would drive the curriculum? What community would serve as a focal point for CUME's future development? Would CUME have the future it wanted or the future it would be given by its parent partner?

CUTS and CUME learned that each partner in an urban ministry program must, in some way, be vulnerable to the failure of the program if the program is to reach its potential. It is a valuable lesson that demands shared equality of outcomes in models of innovative urban ministry partnerships. It is a lesson that is still in process in faith-based partnership initiatives.

Curriculum

Just as the quality of the relationship of an urban ministry program to its community partner is critical to its existence, so is the configuration of the student profile to the design and organization of its curriculum. In urban ministry programs, the clergy or lay participant is as much a part of the curriculum as the textbook and other resource materials. The urban ministry expert in urban ministry programs is not the only instructor. Each student, as an urban ministry practitioner, brings his or her contextualized expertise to the learning environment and helps to transform the collective body through his or her own personal transformation. This learned experience is then transported to the church and community for duplication. The curriculum is always in a process of "discovery," surrounded by an inductive, interactive, informal, and integrative learning cycle. The urban ministry program must always include both teacher and student. It is in the shared capacity to be both a conduit of knowledge and a recipient of knowledge that the urban ministry program models for its student the flexibility of fluidity required for more effective learning.

In giving attention to andragogy, a theory of adult learning that perceives learning as a process of active inquiry rather than passive reception of transmitted content, an urban ministry program honors the learner's experience as the highest tribute in the learning process. As it uses this action-reflection methodology, the role of the curriculum in an urban ministry program is to help adult learners enhance their skills for self-directed inquiry. The curriculum also seeks to enhance the capacity of adult learners to integrate the results of their inquiry so that they, and those they serve, experience greater meaning, greater freedom, and greater peace.

Andragogy challenges formerly held concepts of excellence and intelligence measured by traditional education. What is most excellent is the servant who is able to live and love in "a still more excellent way" (1 Cor. 12:31), and contributes to the common good in spite of the temptation to give up when the "powers" advance their war platform. Excellence is an inside experience that moves outward rather than an externally measured experience. Excellence is the increase of the God-self, and the decrease of one's personhood, so that the act of personal transformation serves as the invitation for others to draw nearer to the grace of God. Excellence is not so much what one does, but who one is in the Christ-Spirit.

Within theological schools there is a tension between scholarship and practical instruction. Traditionally, scholarship reigns, and praxis outside of the academy has been devalued. Too many seminaries with traditional worldviews teach urban ministry students as if they were blank slates, without regard for the personhood, ministry, and experience they bring into the classroom. This blatant disrespect causes havoc and sends students out less whole than when they entered. In holding many of these persons hostage to the lure of educational credentials, far too many seminaries miss the opportunity to become co-learners and expand their own servanthood calling. The risk of becoming a partner in this process, however, is that seminaries may discover they need to change in order to become better at what they do. The literature on resistance to change within theological cultures is abundant. Most are reluctant to enter into intentional transformation through a prescribed and visible change process, although this is what they advocate for others. This is a sad commentary given recent surveys that call attention to the "invisible" status of seminaries and theological education in the secular community. The theological education community must realize what others in the secular community have already recognized: that many of the best and most innovative programs serving marginalized communities are run by churches and other faith-based organizations or groups without benefit of seminary input.

Both CUTS and CUME housed in the center of their curriculum a contextualized methodology with a strong emphasis on Bible and theology. The emphasis that CUTS and CUME placed on attending to the felt need of its students was appropriate. Both of these programs embraced competencies over sequential and rote learning. Both shunned the reward of memorized and regurgitated course content for a grade as evidence of learning, focusing instead on the student's ability to integrate theory and practice as a sign of growth. Both knew that adult learners do not seek to learn simply to know, but seek to know in order to learn how to do. Substantial evidence on adult learning supports the theory that adults learn best when their time is respected and they can see a direct correlation between what they are learning and what they are doing. CUTS and CUME realized that it is in the doing that the knowing finds its meaning for these learners. Seminaries that insist upon the knowing as future investment for the possibility of doing frequently fail to teach these learners because they miss them in the "now." It is to CUTS's and CUME's credit that they recognized the centrality of the "now" moment for urban ministry–based theological education. Unfortunately, CUTS experienced programmatic trauma when it failed to shift into the fullness of the "now" moment as demanded by its changing student population. The changing needs of the newer students appeared to grind against the reluctance of the leadership to massage its vision to accommodate an expanding identity.

In shaping an urban ministry–contextualized curriculum with a strong biblical and theological focus, the goal is for all of the parts to fit together to make up the whole. The leadership, the faculty, the "text-book" contribution present in each student, the course content, the reading material, the time, day, and location of the course, the respect and relationship of peers, the culture of the collective body, and the ethos of the teaching/learning milieu all blend to make an artful presentation. The omission of any critical component affects the rhythm and authenticity of the whole. The rhythm, one of shared give-and-take, celebrates the message, "I am because you are, you are because I am. Together we are better than either of us alone. Let's keep working at this until we get it right . . . we only have each other." Naturally, as with any artistic expression, this kind of art form requires sufficient space for respect, patience, humility, genuine care, forgiveness, and other gifts of the Spirit to be nurtured and modeled.

As educational brokers and entrepreneurs, CUTS and CUME ushered in vital laboratory settings that addressed a critical dialogue in theological education: What is the role of seminaries in working with experienced Christian church leaders from marginalized communities, many with solid ministerial backgrounds, who bring enormous gifts, wisdom, and savvy into their seminary? This question is as pressing today as it was when CUTS and CUME began their urban ministry journey. CUTS and CUME demonstrated that the "invisible" adult learner, shadowed in the traditional theological setting, becomes visible and valued as a co-participant in the urban ministry learning environment; in this process he or she becomes not only an effective learner, but a more effective ministry leader.

This is the crowning accomplishment of CUTS and CUME. Clearly, neither has accomplished all that it set out to do. What is noteworthy, however, is that each set out, at times against the odds, to craft a more just opportunity for traditionally marginalized urban church leaders to receive a sound theological education. Because of the success of these programs it is impossible for the theological education community to utilize only one lens in designing theological education for the contemporary urban ministry student. Both programs demonstrated that the risk they took on behalf of the marginalized honors the biblical mandate to loose the bonds, break the yoke, and help the oppressed to set themselves free. Each program proved that people who do not participate in their own liberation remain forever bound. The action-reflection methodology brilliantly offers persons, excluded from traditional theological education constraints, the freedom to boldly and aggressively say "yes" to their God-self, the Christ-Spirit within, and the very core of their humanity.

Twenty-five years ago when seminary students were driven by abstract learning, the students in CUTS and CUME were learning from their work, action, and reflection. Traditional theological education is now beginning to shift and embrace non-traditional educational models. Our thanks go to CUTS and CUME for being good stewards of the mission to provide theological education and ministry training for the under-represented, and for challenging theological education to liberate itself from its prison of abstraction.

Commentary

ROGER S. GREENWAY

At one point in the CUME case, a staff member looked at the direction the program had taken and asked: "Is this what we really want? Is this what Scripture demands? Is this what the Lord wants?" He was asking the right questions, and I believe the right answer to all three was "No." The reason, as I will explain, is that marrying the "academy" to the inner city community usually produces unhappy families and dysfunctional children. The following comments will explain what I mean.

A Common Vision

Programs like CUTS and CUME begin with a marvelous vision. The founders aim at strengthening inner-city churches and their communities by providing contextualized education for church leaders. The focus is on inner-city people and their needs. Links with educational institutions outside the inner city are meant to help achieve the primary goal. No one imagines that the outside links may someday threaten to turn the programs away from the initial vision. But the founders underestimate the power of academic institutions to control whoever and whatever comes under their umbrellas. They forget the old adage: *If you go to bed with an elephant you are liable to be squashed.*

The Nature of the "Academy"

For our purposes here, I will call the "academy" everything that is part of the formal post-graduate model of ministerial training — degrees, accreditation, faculty with Ph.D.'s, tenure, libraries, curriculum, the works. My comments about the "academy" may seem harsh. However, they are not meant to discredit the value of formal education. It is a

123

source of strength to the church and its mission in the world. Nor are these remarks intended to place theologians and other scholars in a bad light. Christianity needs scholars of the highest order, and the cause of the gospel would be set back without them.

The problem is that the "academy" has not proven to be a friend to inner-city churches. It is not because academicians are callous people who have no concern for minorities or compassion for the poor. Guardians of the "academy" do not intentionally set out to prevent the marginalized from enjoying the benefits of higher theological education. It is simply that the "academy" and inner-city churches move in very different social and cultural worlds. They operate by different standards and pursue goals that lead in different directions. The "academy" expects courses to fit traditional curriculums even though they do not meet the perceived needs of inner-city leaders. The "academy" insists that faculty appointees meet standards set by communities far removed from the inner city. The "academy" requires substantial libraries and an array of things that inner-city institutions cannot provide. When inner-city training programs become dependent on outside institutions in order to maintain standards defined by the "academy," these programs experience continual pressure to submit to the "academy's" direction-setting control, with the result that the programs become less and less helpful to inner-city people.

The Making of Inner-City Leaders

Something to be admired about great inner-city churches is the way their leaders balance the three essential qualities of Christian leadership: godly character, ministerial skills, and knowledge of Scripture. By the standards set by the "academy," many of these leaders are deficient in certain areas of knowledge such as church history, Greek, Hebrew, and other subjects found in the curriculums of traditional seminaries. However, the inner-city leaders are men and women of integrity, they love God and have a passion for ministry, and people follow them most of all for who they *are*.

The expectation of this kind of spiritual servant-leadership is deeply ingrained in almost all inner-city congregations. Inner-city church members expect in their pastors godliness and commitment to ministry, and these qualities are far more important to them than academic credentials. I recognize that many inner-city leaders desire to obtain the benefits of accredited seminary education. But this is valid so long as the priorities that inner-city churches instinctively cherish are protected.

The "academy" puts KNOWLEDGE first, allowing ministry skills and godly character to tag behind. Inner-city churches put character first, skills second, and knowledge third. They want leaders who first of all are people of mature Christian character, have demonstrated faithfulness and proficiency in ministry, and possess a sufficient knowledge of Scripture and theology to feed the minds and hearts of inner-city people. The all-too-common reordering of these priorities under the pressures of seminary curriculum is a curse that inner-city churches should avoid at all costs.

One way to avoid the problem is to keep insisting, as CUTS and CUME did at the outset, that students enrolled in the programs already be active leaders in their churches and that they continue to serve the churches as long as they are enrolled. It is the local church that best molds character and allows ministry gifts to be expressed and evaluated. Diligence in prayer, wisdom and discernment, eagerness to serve others, power in preaching and evangelism, and the ability to exercise authority while maintaining a humble attitude are the most important qualities in Christian leaders. But the "academy" does little to contribute to their development and sometimes it does them damage.

Andragogy versus Pedagogy

When CUTS and CUME began, most students were church leaders, many of them pastors who were mature men and women rich in experience both in Christian ministry and in the workplace. These students were bi-vocational to begin with, since they served congregations and supported themselves through full-time secular employment. In a sense they became tri-vocational when they added weekly hours in the classroom to their busy schedules. Only highly motivated adults accept such challenges.

The educational approach that best serves adults of this kind is not pedagogy (etymologically, *teaching children*), but andragogy *(teaching*

125

adults). Andragogy operates with a different set of rules, and it is the most effective way to teach adults, especially highly motivated, experienced adults such as those enrolled at CUTS and CUME. However, pedagogical methods predominate among schools connected to the "academy." In my estimation, herein lies a major problem. How do you wed the expectations of traditional accrediting associations with the character and needs of inner-city adult learners?

In an article entitled "Seven Characteristics of Highly Effective Adult Learning Programs," Dorothy D. Billington tells of her recent findings as to the type of learning environment that best helps adults grow and develop.[1] Her research reinforces earlier studies done by Malcolm Knowles regarding the superiority of andragogical methods to traditional pedagogical approaches when mature and motivated students are involved. Billington's research reveals that adults can and do experience significant personal growth when the training is in *one type of learning environment*. But they tended not to grow, or even to regress, in another type of environment. The seven key factors found in effective adult learning programs are:

1. Students feel safe, respected, and supported; their individual needs are met and their abilities and life achievements are acknowledged.
2. There is freedom to think on their own, experiment, create, and pursue what interests them.
3. Faculty treats students as adults and peers, and students are shown respect as intelligent people with valuable insights gained by a variety of educational experiences.
4. There is self-directed learning, and students are expected to take responsibility for much of their own learning. They work with faculty to design learning programs that fit their needs and interests.
5. There is "pacing" in the educational process, which means students are challenged just beyond their current level of ability, not so far ahead as to discourage them nor behind so as to bore them.
6. Students and instructors dialogue a great deal; students tell of the

---

1. Dorothy D. Billington, "Seven Characteristics of Highly Effective Adult Learning Programs," in *The Adult Learner in Higher Education and the Workplace* (Seattle: New Horizons for Learning, 2000), pp. 1-3.

new ideas they hear in the workplace, and these are discussed and evaluated.

7. Faculty responds to students' input as to what they need and how they learn best. Curriculum and teaching styles are adapted accordingly.

In contrast, says Billington, where adult students feel they are regarded as ignorant underlings, their life achievements are given scant attention, and their individual needs are not taken seriously, they tend to regress, their self-confidence is undermined, and they develop very little. Evidence points to the fact that student-centered educational programs are far superior to faculty-centered programs when applied to the type of students CUTS and CUME serve. However, the "academy" and the andragogical approach to teaching do not get along well. Programs like CUTS and CUME have made valiant efforts to make good use of andragogical insights, but the closer the accreditors come, the more nervous everyone gets.

Suggestions

New Accrediting Associations

The time has come to give serious consideration to the formation of new accrediting associations that will respect the value of andragogical teaching methods and alternative paths to ministerial training. It seems to me that many undergraduate schools are more responsive to the needs and wants of inner-city people. Many Christian colleges are putting forth solid efforts to place undergraduate education within reach of minority students, and their efforts are to be commended. But at the post-graduate level where most seminaries operate, I am not convinced that the rigid standards and traditions of "academia" can be stretched enough to meet the needs of marginalized communities. Therefore, I believe that inner-city church leaders ought to give serious consideration to forming new accrediting organizations designed to enhance, monitor, and credential education for ministry in inner-city communities.

Following Andragogical Principles

Recently, I was discussing contextualized theological education in the Central American setting with a Christian educator from Costa Rica. He described how the Evangelical University of Costa Rica offers full academic credit to two programs, one that focuses on theological education and the other on missionary training, both of which follow andragogical principles in the training they offer. Our discussion centered around the concept of a "credit," and of a "credited course," which the university in Costa Rica defines as 45 hours of work (15 hours in class and 30 hours of practical ministry) that is assigned, supervised, and evaluated by an approved professor. In addition to approved professors, most of whom are bi-vocational, the program makes use of adjunct instructors in extension centers for supervising the students' practical work. Courses, whatever their title in the curriculum, are student-centered and outcome-based. Distance between study and ministry is shortened. The operation of the program is largely self-sustaining. Tuition covers the wages of professors and adjuncts, and church offerings and donations cover administrative costs. Funds for buildings are raised through development campaigns.

The need for fresh initiatives is enormous. For example, my own denomination (the Christian Reformed Church in North America) now worships in twenty-two different languages each Sunday, but the denominational seminary can serve only a fraction of these different groups. I suggest that partnerships be formed between city pastors, lay church leaders, and individual seminary professors for the purpose of producing new forms of ministerial training that draw from the strengths of the various traditions and offer multiethnic churches what they need and want. To safeguard the programs from outside control, the governing boards must be firmly in the hands of inner-city and minority leaders. If evangelicals can do creative, contextualized education in Costa Rica, what prevents us from "pushing the envelope" further in North America? Maybe "academia" can change.

Commentary

RICHARD WHITE

If a community is a collection of people united around common goals, then institutions are those vehicles created by the community to achieve shared purposes, be they educational, commercial, industrial, recreational, cultural, or religious.

> HAROLD DERIENZO,
> "Beyond the Melting Pot, Preserving Culture,
> Building Community," *National Civic Review* (Winter 1995)

[I]n America our zest for quality education — and the ponderous institutions that have grown up with that goal — has hammered out a system which tends to filter out the truly gifted leaders in our local churches. It is the old story of what is easier for the doctor rather than what is easier for the patient.

> RALPH WINTER,
> "Editorial Comment,"
> *Mission Frontiers Bulletin* 20 (March-April 1998): 3-4

Theological Apartheid[1]

These case studies are stories about how the cultures, social structures, and guiding beliefs of two different communities — traditional seminary-based institutions and non-traditional neighborhood-based[2] in-

1. Cf. Douglas S. Massey and Nancy A. Denton, *American Apartheid: Segregation and the Making of the Underclass* (Cambridge, Mass.: Harvard University Press, 1993).
2. I have chosen to use this term rather than "community-based" to avoid confusion with the use of the term "community" throughout this article. I use

129

stitutions — affect the delivery of theological education. As stories, they are messy, lack precision, and their uniqueness threatens their generalizability, yet they help us understand some of the complexities of urban theological education (Forester, 1999).

CUME and CUTS act as mediating institutions between the grassroots community with which they identify and the academic community upon whom they depend for resources (Neuhaus and Berger, 1990). They buffer the negative effects of large institutions on vulnerable populations, and they act as a conduit for the flow of information and resources between the traditional and the non-traditional theological programs. Consequently, they experience the tension of relating to two relatively isolated communities. This, coupled with the resource advantage of traditional theological institutions, tends to force curriculum into a structural and procedural conformity we might call academic orthodoxy (cf. Guiness, 1984; Hackney, 1993; Winter, 1998).

Curriculum development for urban ministry training flows from our understanding of community and our belief about whether models of contextualization should be dominated by one community or the other. As one informant said, the clash between traditional and non-traditional programs appears "to center around the basic underlying educational philosophy that would drive curriculum, specifically *which community* was going to serve as the overall focal point."

Social scientists suggest that there are two basic types of community: interest and location (Godfrey, 1988). The first is organized around a common outlook, the second around a common location. In both, community solidarity is dependent on the quality of relationship and a sustained interaction. Community members' destinies are linked to the extent that they share a common view of life, hold similar values, and participate together in many institutions (Perry, 1987). One might suppose that traditional and non-traditional programs, in spite of their different locations, would function as a community of interest, since they share the common goal of theological education. But I suggest they are, in fact, separate and isolated. One community is primarily an advantaged, relatively powerful and wealthy, white-dominated, and largely suburban population. The other is a disadvantaged, relatively

---

neighborhood-based to signify institutions whose culture, structure, and processes reflect the locality in which they are embedded.

powerless, low-income and working-class, non-white, and inner-urban population. The question is whether we might create a community held together "by shared understandings and a sense of [mutual] obligation" (Bender, 1978).

CUME and CUTS have created a more-or-less permanent neighborhood presence among poor and working-class populations. As the cases indicate, both emerged in the 1970s in response to a clearly identified need for theological education specifically contextualized to the inner city. Both attempt to address the needs "of those cut off from wider society that demands recognized credentials," and "those denied a theological education primarily due to the lack of prior educational experience."

Building Theological Capital

In the language of community development, they attempt to build theological capital. We are familiar with the development of political and economic capital, the process of accumulating power and financial advantage. Human capital is the knowledge and skill people build through school, apprenticeships, and training. Individuals with greater human capital tend to achieve greater lifetime earnings. Social capital refers to the resources embedded in individual and organizational relationships — social networks — that make communities more livable (Putnam, 1995). Communities with greater social capital tend to experience better social health and fewer social ills. Theological education introduces students to the concepts and tools that allow them to think critically and act with confidence in ministry. The purpose of building theological capital is, as someone else has said, "to *form* church leaders among God's people, to *inform* them about their faith and its application to modern life; so that they may become agents of *transformation*."

It is relatively easy for individuals born into an environment of accumulated political, economic, human, social, and theological capital to generate more. Conversely, individuals born into disadvantaged environments, like those served by CUME and CUTS, tend to experience disadvantage along more than one dimension. Consequently, theological training is more difficult and more costly for the disadvantaged to obtain (cf. McIntosh, 1988). Building theological capital requires building other forms of capital as well.

Donald Gardner of CUTS identified these costs: "We help many students get high school equivalency who then go on to attain degrees. All this takes time, individual tutoring, special assistance, and encouragement." This approach is "labor intensive" and "costly in terms of dollars, time, and energy." Traditional programs of theological education take for granted the existence of other forms of capital and tend to concentrate resources on developing theological capital alone. But in disadvantaged communities, theological education is not easily separated from building political, economic, human, and social capital.

Socio-Cultural Distance

That the director and staff of CUME believed "the distance between the two campuses was not a hindrance" indicates their failure to recognize, or at least to articulate, the gulf that exists in the thinking of traditional and non-traditional models of theological education symbolized in geography. As long as the distance in geography or educational philosophy keeps either institution *isolated* from the other, it will be a hindrance. Accessibility to centers of power and decision-making is important. Geography matters.

Healthy communities are marked by a high degree of citizen participation (Berry et al., 1993). Communities where citizens are given the opportunity to identify their own issues and problems, create plans to address those issues, and are able to implement those plans tend to be healthier (cf. Berry et al., 1993; Levine and Perkins, 1997; and Kretzman and McKnight, 1993). Disadvantaged communities have little voice in decisions that affect the quality of their daily lives. Seminary-based theological education, like most higher education, tends to be hierarchical. Faculty, administration, and governing boards typically make critical decisions; student contributions tend to be limited to satisfaction surveys and anecdotal stories. Vulnerability of the disadvantaged community is increased by reducing their participation in the design and implementation of neighborhood-based theological education.

Whether seminary-based or neighborhood-based, quality theological education requires expanding the range of opportunities for participation in decision-making and making that participation more meaningful. A 1994 study by the M. J. Murdock Charitable Trust discovered that church leaders believe the seminary is the best source for education in biblical, theological, historical, and language training, but not in training for leadership in the local congregation, understanding subcultures, or deepening spiritual life. Community ownership through collaborative decision-making increases the likelihood of curriculum relevancy and institutional sustainability, especially in disadvantaged communities.

Although the mission of both types of institution is to prepare men and women for Christian leadership and ministry in the city, how that mission is enacted is quite different. The students, faculty, and staff of the seminary and the non-traditional programs not only serve separate communities, they *are* separate communities. Note, for example, the Park Street Church site of Gordon-Conwell's new urban programs. "The church drew most of its congregation from suburban communities and included people who were of some influence in the city's business, government, and professional sectors." The difference in physical location is highlighted by the advantage of wealth, power, and prestige. *Sub*urban versus *inner*-urban, advantaged versus disadvantaged, diffuse versus compact. The naïve concern of seminary faculty whether "persons of color were able to master the biblical languages" underscores the fact that these are not only separate but isolated communities.[3]

Cultural isolation is not unique to theological education. In 1995, reporters at a national conference considering clinical trials of an AIDS vaccine witnessed fragmentation among participants who all cared passionately about the subject. "Try as they might to work together, the groups *speak different languages*. The scientists 'present' their information while the community representatives 'share' theirs. . . . [T]he language conflict is trivial compared to the *conflict of culture*" (Green, 1995, emphasis added). The academicians were considered "ivory-tower do-

---

3. The history of rural/urban bias in the U.S. affects the way we view inner-urban neighborhoods (e.g., Lewis's *Culture of Poverty,* or the writing of Durkheim, Tonnies, and Wirth). A popular myth asserts that they arise from social disorganization and limited intellectual capacity that keep them from achieving the "American Dream" epitomized in suburban ranchettes and upscale townhouses.

nothings" who were "remote from the world of suffering." Community representatives were thought to "represent no one but themselves." Even in matters of life and death, the cultural distance between two communities who are otherwise focused on the same issue can seem insurmountable.

Academic Orthodoxy and Theological Relevancy

If we can frame the discussion of community in terms of the advantaged and the disadvantaged, we can frame the discussion of curriculum in terms of academic orthodoxy and theological relevancy (Guiness, 1984). In the extreme, academic orthodoxy sacrifices relevancy to avoid compromising the content and quality of theological education. It is akin to fears of syncretism associated with contextualization of the gospel (Hesselgrave and Rommen, 1989). Don Gardner of CUTS noted that some staff and adjunct faculty "considered real ministry to be evangelism, preaching, and teaching." They were "uneasy about curriculum changes . . . that incorporated concrete preparation for life/work skills." Westminster courses and the process for approval of curricular changes were protracted. At CUME, "students who want to take just one course were frustrated because we mostly offer courses that meet degree requirements." CUME's Assistant Director of Student Advisement also voiced this frustration when she asked whether the curriculum continued to serve CUME's target communities if it emphasized degree completion programs at the expense of its certificate programs.

CUME and CUTS are pressured by the institutions upon which they depend for resources to reflect the interests of traditional theological education, namely to grant degrees. To be fair, there is pressure on the seminary from constituents who look for tangible products and accreditation associations that guard the quality of that product. But when seminaries retain absolute control of resources, the curriculum, buildings, staff, and faculty of non-traditional programs are held for ransom and amount to assets that, though they are *within* the community, are controlled from *outside* the community (cf. Kretzman and McKnight, 1993). Power does not have to be coercive to have a coercive effect (Domhoff, 1979, 1990).

Unfortunately, as the cases demonstrate, unilateral resource control results in a loss of relevancy for the non-traditional student. This is analogous to spatial mismatch in urban economics — high unemployment among inner-urban populations resulting from the suburbanization of industry or as a result of entry-level jobs that do not match the education and skills of inner-urban residents. The lack of collaboration between inner-urban and industrial leadership results in economic vulnerability and further disadvantage. Similarly, academic orthodoxy leads to a community-curriculum mismatch for the disadvantaged when the curriculum is suburbanized and not relevant to the inner-urban cultural milieu.

As secular models of higher education demonstrate, the fear that contextualization of the curriculum will result in a loss of academic quality is unfounded. Portland State University, whose motto is *Doctrina Urbi Serviati* — Let Knowledge Serve the City — and the University of California, Santa Cruz, can serve as good examples of contextualized higher education. The educational product of PSU must be justified in the light of its mission "to enhance urban life through education, research, and public service." Non-credentialed "community faculty" and student field-experience are utilized throughout the curriculum. Seniors, working in teams, are required to complete a collaborative year-long capstone course with a community-based organization where their knowledge and skills are brought to bear on a specific urban problem. Similarly, for more than twenty-five years, the University of California, Santa Cruz, has required students to complete a six-month field study with community organizations "that make a difference," then return to campus for their final year before they can graduate with a degree in community studies (Lawson, 1994).

A shift away from academic orthodoxy toward a similar community-focused, reflection-action-reflection educational model could address the concerns of both the traditional and non-traditional theological student and help close the gap between them. As noted above, church leadership believes traditional seminary education is sound, but that it also fails to provide a cultural understanding or the skills necessary for urban ministry.

Gordon-Conwell's "redefinition of the urban education concept and the forecast of new student markets among international students and marketplace workers" is a step in this direction. However, this transition must be made without creating another institution for the advantaged at the expense of relevant theological education for the disadvantaged. The guiding force behind any shift in the structure of curriculum must be a desire to improve the overall quality of theological education, not merely an attempt to break open new markets. If traditional urban theological programs are to make this shift to a collaborative, hands-on, interactive, reflection-action-reflection curriculum, it will take leadership at the top who will persevere in the face of opposition. Non-traditional institutions cannot resist the crushing force of academic orthodoxy by themselves. Gordon-Conwell's approach frankly requires fewer resources and less risk than working with the disadvantaged. If we treat the development of theological education as simply a fine-tuning and gap-filling exercise for academic orthodoxy, we limit our view. We put the considerable accomplishments of programs like CUME and CUTS at risk, and ignore, at our peril, the opportunity to come to grips with addressing concerns of the city, ultimately increasing the isolation and vulnerability of the disadvantaged.

At its worst, academic orthodoxy encourages a focus on narrowly defined tasks, offers narrowly defined answers to complex issues, and treats non-traditional students as clients or consumers of services rather than as *participants* in the evolution of ideas and projects that form the common life of the city. There is little hope of creating a community held together by shared understanding and a sense of mutual obligation without true collaboration between the seminary- and neighborhood-based institutions. Without common focus, participatory decision-making, and a sense of common destiny, there is no community. The ambivalence over degree programs and accreditation presented in the two case studies is embedded in the tension that results when CUME and CUTS attempt to preserve resources for the community that are largely controlled from outside the community.

In the end, curriculum hinges on how we resolve the community question. Will the non-traditional institution be allowed to reflect the culture, social fabric, and religious ethos of the community in which it is embedded, or must it conform to the seminary on which it depends for its existence?

The breadth, depth, and design of any curriculum must respond to the students. An academic administrator of a large metropolitan alternative school that serves students in special education, drop-out recovery, substance abuse rehabilitation, and students who have been abandoned by the school system recently noted, "teaching is simply responding to how your students learn. If you are unwilling to adjust your methods to their ways of learning, then you simply aren't teaching."[4]

Underlying Assumptions and Courses of Action

May I suggest two underlying assumptions of my argument and three courses of action to address these issues. First, resolution of the community question begins by recognizing that divisions of race and class in the U.S. are deep. The divisions cleave the church and the seminary as well. Those engaged in theological education must admit there are two distinct communities, one advantaged, one disadvantaged. If I understand the example of Christ, it falls upon the advantaged to make a way for the disadvantaged. If we fail to address these inequities of ethnic and cultural apartheid in theological education, then we lose an opportunity to speak and act prophetically to the rest of our nation.

Second, we must recognize that non-traditional students start with a different set of assets and liabilities. It makes no sense to address only one dimension of the complex of theological education. To accomplish this, I suggest, the seminary must take into account the forms of capital it takes for granted. The neighborhood-based programs must inventory their assets and liabilities — including the latent assets of community life that have not been fully explored. A comparison of the two inventories should reveal biases and guide the development of curriculum relevant for both. Theological education is not a zero-sum game.

Related to the above, the structure and process of theological education must shift in three important areas to reflect our changing world. First, decision-making must become less hierarchical and more collaborative. This will help address the increasing need for flexibility and community ownership. Curriculum must respond to student and community needs in order to ensure program sustainability. Lasting programs are owned by communities that sense their fingerprints are on the product.

A lessening of the curriculum/community mismatch requires a reduction in isolation. Structures and processes that intentionally

4. A highly qualified educational consultant, my wife.

bring the two communities together must be put in place (cf. Berry et al.). Secular models of higher education demonstrate that this does not result in a loss of content, but increases student apprehension of the subject. This will require collaboration and cooperation that is equitable and the acceptance of "community faculty" whose credentials are not necessarily academic.

Third, program evaluation and assessment procedures must reflect an orientation toward the community rather than an orientation toward accreditation associations and financial backers. This is admittedly risky, but sound intellectual arguments supported by extant quantitative and qualitative research rather than a corporate cost-benefit approach should be used.

If the purpose of urban ministerial education is to develop Christian leadership well equipped to meet the demands of city ministry, then the embedded issues of accessibility and relevancy must be addressed. This is not just a matter of meeting the needs of disadvantaged communities, as we have seen, but it is also a matter of quality education for the traditional student as well. As Don Gardner of CUTS noted, "theology is best done in praxis. The church must understand its community context so that it can be an effective agent for justice in the community through a biblically sound, spiritually invigorating, and socially transforming ministry."

Bibliography

Bender, Thomas. *Community and Social Change in America.* New Brunswick, N.J.: Rutgers University Press, 1978.

Berger, Peter L., and Richard John Neuhaus. "To Empower People: The Role of Mediating Structures in Public Policy." Edited by David Giles, J. Steven Ott, and Jay M. Shafritz. *The Nonprofit Organization: Essential Readings.* Pacific Grove, Calif.: Brooks/Co., 1990.

Berry, Jeffrey M., Kent E. Portneyt, and Ken Thompson. *The Rebirth of Urban Democracy.* Washington, D.C.: The Bookings Institution, 1993.

Domhoff, G. William. *The Powers That Be: Processes of Ruling-Class Domination in America.* New York: Random House, 1979.

———. *The Power Elite and the State: How Policy Is Made in America.* New York: Aldine, 1990.

Forester, John. *The Deliberative Practitioner.* Cambridge, Mass.: MIT Press, 1999.

Godfrey, Brian J. *Neighborhoods in Transition: The Making of San Francisco's Ethnic and Nonconformist Communities.* Berkeley: University of California Press, 1988.

Greene, Joel. "Who Put the Lid on gp120?" *New York Times Magazine,* March 26, 1995.

Guiness, Os. *The Gravedigger File: Papers on the Subversion of the Modern Church.* Downers Grove, Ill.: InterVarsity Press, 1984.

Hackney, Sheldon. "Reinventing American Universities to Overcome the Problem of the City." Paper delivered at the Conference on Universities and the City, University of Pennsylvania, June 23, 1993.

Hesselgrave, David J., and Edward Rommen. *Contextualization, Meanings, Methods, and Models.* Grand Rapids: Baker, 1989.

Kretzman, John, and John McKnight. *Building Communities from the Inside Out.* Evanston, Ill.: Northwestern University, 1993.

Lawson, Jered. "The Well-Trained Practical Idealist." *RAIN* 14, no. 4 (Summer 1994): 43-51.

Levine, Murray, and David V. Perkins. *Principles of Community Psychology,* 2nd Edition. New York: Oxford University Press, 1997.

Massey, Douglas S., and Nancy A. Denton. *American Apartheid: Segregation and the Making of the Underclass.* Cambridge, Mass.: Harvard University Press, 1993.

McIntosh, Peggy. "White Privilege and Male Privilege," in Anderson and Collins, eds., *Race, Class, and Gender.* Belmont, Mass.: Wadsworth, 1988.

———. *Review of Graduate Theological Education in the Pacific Northwest.* Vancouver, Wash.: The M. J. Murdock Charitable Trust, 1994.

Perry, Stewart E. *Communities on the Way.* New York: State University of New York Press, 1987.

Putnam, Robert. "Bowling Alone: America's Declining Social Capital," *Journal of Democracy* 6, no. 1 (January 1995): 65-78.

Winter, Ralph. "Editorial Comment." *Mission Frontiers Bulletin* 20 (March-April 1998): 3-4.

Case Study: Whose Program Is It?

The Seminary Consortium for Urban Pastoral Education's board meeting was just a week away. Executive Director Andrew Niemann wondered how many more — or rather, how few — meetings might follow. After a significant decline in student enrollment, from 35 in its heyday to 5 the previous year, the board had shut down for one year its core program — an experiential and academic off-campus year for seminary students. SCUPE's tenth biennial Congress on Urban Ministry had occurred several months ago. No firm plans had been made yet for the next congress — nor grant commitments received. After twenty years of cooperative theological education for urban ministry, was it time to close up shop, as most similar programs had over the years?

Andrew had used the year off from directing the urban theological studies program to focus on the decline in enrollment and to explore future possibilities. He and SCUPE's staff had structured a series of three consultations with the deans of both member and non-member seminaries to see what insight they had into falling enrollment and what remedies they had to offer. Wrestling with which recommendations to bring to the board meeting, Andrew reflected on the consultations and tried to gauge SCUPE's chances for survival.

*   *   *

This case was written by David J. Frenchak and Mark S. R. Walden. The names of all persons have been disguised to protect their privacy.

Andrew had begun each of the consultations by sharing the early history and founding of the Consortium:

> SCUPE came into existence to meet a need for educated and trained leadership to serve urban churches.
>
> The founding schools wanted a leadership development program, not an exposure program. SCUPE was designed to provide professional education in how to do community exegesis and community development; to equip pastors with an understanding of urban systems and issues; and to introduce tools for political, sociological, and theological analysis.
>
> Since we began, SCUPE has had over 400 students go through its urban ministry leadership development program. We have served fifteen different seminaries and have alumni in cities all over the world. From the perspective of the city and the urban church, the need for such leadership is every bit as strong today as it was when SCUPE was created. Can we address the apparent lack of interest among students, as well as the structural difficulties at the seminary, so that we can meet the need evidenced not only in Chicago but in numerous cities, large and small?

Andrew recalled that discussion began immediately. Demographics seemed to be an easy place for the seminary representatives to dig in. They described how their student body had changed substantially since SCUPE began twenty years ago. First, there was a drop in student enrollment. Second, the makeup of the student body now looked very different. Students were older, with many entering second or third careers.

Most students were also married, many with children. With working spouses and children in school, they were no longer able to move easily. Students seemed much more intent on getting through seminary quickly, particularly the second-career students. The weight of student loans was mentioned by a number of faculty persons as burdening their students. Given fewer students, decreased mobility, and increased orientation toward the fast track to graduation and career, there was little wonder why off-campus study programs did not fare well.

SCUPE's program director, Kathleen O'Connor, queried: "My understanding is that when SCUPE began, many seminary students were being called immediately upon graduation to serve urban churches with little or no academic or experiential preparation. Is this still the case? Where does urban ministry fit into the vocational picture for both incoming and graduating students?"

There was a silence; then Anthony Hutchinson, dean of a member school, said with a touch of regret: "It is important that we understand this is the late nineties, not the late sixties. Urban ministry neither has the appeal it once did, nor is it a place recent graduates are often called. It does not seem to be high on the agenda of incoming students, nor do they see such a focus as important to their careers."

"Perhaps with one exception," volunteered Steven Schwarz, dean of another member seminary. "We have a lot more women in our student body, and they seem to be more interested in mission and urban ministry."

"That's because frequently that's the only place they can expect a call," interjected Janice Ingram, field education director at a non-member school. "The truth is, our male-dominated denomination is more interested in the megachurch than in urban ministry. If SCUPE could combine the two, you would have more students than you could handle."

Andrew wondered whether she was joking or serious about the possibility of integrating the suburban-oriented megachurch model into the diversity of the city.

Lars Johnson, dean of a member school, gave some good critical input: "The problem of a lack of students cannot be totally understood by demographic changes," he began. "For us it is a structural problem. The SCUPE program is eleven months — that's a big chunk of time. Our students are required to take a number of courses, often in sequence. If a student leaves campus for a whole year, it wreaks havoc with the system in place on campus. Seminary programs of study don't have the flexibility to accommodate off-campus studies the way colleges do, at least not our school. About the only way students can do off-campus study is to add another year to their program. None of our students who do SCUPE are able to complete their requirements in three years. Added to that, they use up all of their electives by coming to Chicago for a year and end up paying for more credits than necessary for graduation."

Taking another tack, Professor Linda Christensen from a non-member school ventured, "What does the consortium offer for laity? We have a growing number of people in our denomination who would be interested in urban ministry the way I hear you talking about it, but these folk don't want to become ordained ministers. Perhaps the consortium could offer a degree program or courses for laity."

Lincoln Bradshaw, an African-American faculty person from one of SCUPE's founding member schools, spoke up. "It seems to me," he asserted, "that the course of studies offered by SCUPE is ideal for working pastors, particularly from the African-American church. Maybe we should recruit students from that source, rather than from the seminary campus, since it seems seminary students, faculty, and administrators all lack the time, the interest, and the energy to take urban ministry seriously."

Kathleen recalled for the group a comment by an African-American pastor on Chicago's South Side. "SCUPE's courses," he had said, "are one of the best-kept secrets from the African-American church. Why are we teaching seminary students, the majority of them white, how to be effective agents of transformation in the city — but not teaching these same skills to those already in the pastorate? Many of these pastors could also benefit from some type of academic credentialing."

"I'm not sure SCUPE has the resources to go in that direction," responded Mark Coleman of a non-member Chicago seminary. "We're trying to do that sort of thing on our campus, and it really takes quite an investment. Now I hear that we may be in jeopardy with the Association of Theological Schools because we have a few too many students in some courses who do not have an accredited B.A. degree. My suggestion is that SCUPE not compete with existing programs — and if you do go in this direction, that you go real slow."

"If SCUPE is going to go in the direction of providing educational programs for urban pastors, then we have to find a way to make SCUPE portable. I'm getting pressure from administration and faculty that we are not involved enough in Grand Rapids. Maybe instead of sending students to Chicago, we should send them to the city nearest our campus." It was Allen Dykema, dean of a member seminary. He had been on the job less than a year, but clearly had come with an agenda and a challenge. He continued, "We are really interested in whether SCUPE can help integrate urban ministry into the core curriculum, so that all our students benefit, not just those who decide to come to Chicago. Unless

SCUPE can help us in these two areas, I'm not sure we will stay as members."

SCUPE's director of development, Richard Churchill, asked how new ideas for expanded programs could be funded. It was not easy to raise money for theological education that focused on context rather than a particular church constituency.

Linda Christensen raised another issue. Apart from student and faculty interest in urban ministry and additional program offerings, both her school and denomination had an image problem with SCUPE. "SCUPE," she explained, "is seen as evangelical, and neither our denomination nor our school identifies culturally, politically, or theologically with that image."

"I can't believe it," responded Doug Michelet, who wanted his seminary to join the consortium. "I also think SCUPE has an image problem — but for my school and denomination it is just the opposite. SCUPE is seen as liberal with a heavy emphasis on social justice, talking about transforming not only individuals but social and political systems. Just take a look at the roster of speakers and presenters at SCUPE's last Congress on Urban Ministry. The majority of them were on the political, social, and theological left."

Andrew had heard this conversation before. Theological diversity was a real hot-button. For twenty years he had carried a vision that SCUPE could enable evangelicals with a social conscience and mainline seminaries with a sense of urban mission to connect and talk with each other. The consortium's diverse membership reflected that vision, but it was repeatedly threatened and challenged by students who complained that courses leaned either one way or the other (that is, not the way they leaned), by presidents of the member seminaries concerned that their school's image might be tainted by a sort of theological guilt by association, and by denominational executives who were not at all certain how the ecumenical nature of the consortium related to its mission. Ecumenism no longer seemed to be a strong focus of mainline denominations faced with numerical decline, nor was it valued highly by the more independent and numerically growing evangelicals. Andrew recalled that early in SCUPE's formation, the board had attempted to structure a doctrinal statement, but because of the mixture of theological perspectives represented among them, the founding schools concluded that it was better to have a mission statement as the identifying document.

Andrew defended his vision: "If SCUPE does have an image, I hope it's a bridge. Cities are diverse. We teach that the church can bridge these diversities and become a model for increasing understanding and decreasing physical, economic, and emotional violence. SCUPE itself is a bridge between churches of different theologies and cultures. People from the broadest range of theological perspectives attend our Congress on Urban Ministry. No other national event occurs on a regular basis with such a rich mixture. We also bridge faith communities, cultures, races, languages, social issues, and urban and suburban differences."

"The problem with being a bridge," Richard commented, "is that you get stepped on from both sides."

Andrew chose not to acknowledge the comment and continued,

Part of the genius of SCUPE is that from the beginning we have taken context seriously and are willing to network across theological boundaries. That structural, philosophical, and practical dimension continues to impact our image.

Sociologically, we emphasize systems theory; biblically, we ground our theology of urban ministry in the principalities and powers, understood as both spiritual and structural. This theoretical base and focus are sociologically, politically, and theologically viable for both evangelical and mainline students who take seriously the context of the city as a place to do ministry.

Taking another angle, Allen Dykema made a well-prepared and thought-out statement: "The way I see it, SCUPE's problem with student enrollment began when it was decided that the board of directors would not be constituted of seminary representatives. Since then, you have added programs that have little to do with our seminary's traditional programs. To be perfectly honest, neither our administration nor our faculty feel very much ownership for the consortium or its programs. We have talked about this, and our president is seriously questioning the cost of membership fees, when we're not an integral part of the board's decision-making process and particularly in years when we don't have students in the program."

"I don't understand," Christopher Simms, on faculty at a nonmember seminary, interjected. "You mean as a member school you have

145

to pay for services you don't get? How does this consortium business work?"

Cole Coburn, a faculty member who also served as registrar at his member seminary, responded immediately. "It's even worse," he quickly exclaimed. "We also lose the entire tuition payment of students while they are in this urban program. Institutionally, this is very costly. We frequently have four or five students interested in the SCUPE program, but we only allow two a year to participate."

"Our faculty and administration have also discussed the financial costs of SCUPE membership, and we don't see it that way at all," countered Silvia Gerson-Santos, long-time dean at her member school.

> If we had to set up our own urban program for the three or four students a year who are interested, it would cost us twenty times more than what SCUPE membership costs us. Where else can you get a whole specialized department that includes ten courses, a supervised internship, and a CPE equivalent, for the cost of one on-campus course? We've talked before about the "high" cost of membership, but I simply don't understand the thinking.
>
> As far as being on the board of directors, we have so many faculty committees, I don't need to sit on another one. As long as our faculty is satisfied with the academic quality of the program — and we are — we don't feel a need or a desire to come to more meetings in Chicago. Inviting as this city is in January. I supported the constitutional change saying not every member school had to have a representative on the board of directors back when that was proposed, and our school has had no reason to regret the decision.

There they were, two very different viewpoints, each put on the table by the dean of a founding member school. There were distinct differences in the understandings of governance and economics — and the two issues were linked inseparably.

Andrew, the only person participating in the consultations who was present at SCUPE's founding, recalled the formation of the consortium in 1976. In order to hire a director, the founding schools agreed to fund a pilot project for one year, to hire a consultant to assess the pilot year, and — upon a positive evaluation — to fully fund the program for three years. The founding schools' proposal was presented by three urban pastors who did not want the program dependent on funding from external sources, such as foundations, because it was "soft" money. Andrew agreed to accept the position as director based on the agreement. The pilot project was completed with a very positive evaluation by an independent consultant whose only concern was the limited budget, which he described as "totally unrealistic" and which could "eventually result in the decline of the program's quality and viability."

In 1977, after the successful pilot year, the founding seminaries agreed unanimously that the cooperative program should continue. But after that decision was made, serious conversations took place around financing. Professor Don Wright, substituting for the dean of his school, laid out the case for a decrease in membership fees rather than the increase recommended by the consultant. "Quite frankly," he said, "we cannot afford to pay the price of membership as it is projected for the next three years, and we certainly could not be a member if we voted to raise that amount. While I believe this is a great venture in cooperative theological education, I know for a fact that our president is going to have a difficult time getting this into the school's budget. If we want more member schools, we need to lower, not raise, the membership fees."

Other seminary representatives agreed. "There is a solution to the dilemma," said Professor John Douma. "SCUPE should become a 501(c)(3) educational agency. This would enable it to raise and receive contributions. We need to include fundraising in the job description of the director."

"Good idea," responded Professor David Carlson. "I move that we decrease by half the projected cost of membership for the next three years, that we ask the director to file for 501(c)(3) status, and we instruct the Executive Committee to restructure the director's job description to include fundraising." The motion passed unanimously.

One of the founding urban pastors, recognizing the shift in direction, spoke up. "If we are going to ask the director to raise money, then he needs a board that includes individuals who understand that this is the reason they have been asked to be on the board. As the board is presently structured, everyone is interested in program, not budget. We will need to add lay leaders who can support the organization financially and help the director raise money."

The board agreed and reconstituted itself in three categories: seminary representatives, urban ministry practitioners, and lay persons. The board agreed to meet semi-annually, and the executive committee monthly. For the sake of convenience, the executive committee was composed of Chicago-area board members. All of these, as it turned out, were urban ministry practitioners and lay leaders.

Andrew worked closely with the executive committee, who repeatedly brought to meetings the need for member schools to be more involved in the fundraising activities and budgetary needs of the consortium. However, seminary representatives usually had little power to act on financial affairs that involved their institutions. They were also more interested in program recommendations and preferred to leave financial needs and fundraising concerns to the executive committee. For seminary representatives on the board, raising money for SCUPE seemed like a conflict of interest because the member schools also needed to raise their own funds. As a seminary representative once stated, "isn't that the reason they agreed to add lay leaders to the board of directors?"

Ten years later, with the help of a development consultant, the executive committee recommended a bold change that eliminated the constitutional requirement that each school be represented on the board. The chairperson of the board, an urban pastor who was also the chair of the executive committee, put it this way: "Since SCUPE is an independent 501(c)(3) educational agency that needs to raise its own support, it needs a board fully committed to the task of fundraising." Schools could have representatives on the board, but only if they agreed to accept fundraising responsibilities.

Andrew saw gains and losses in the recommendation. It passed with only mild objection from the seminary representatives, who seemed to feel relief from the need to raise money. Over the years, the director and the board had raised close to two million dollars, enabling SCUPE to become the longest-operating consortium program in urban theological education — and sadly one of very few now remaining. At one time, there were such consortia programs in several cities, including New York, Atlanta, Los Angeles, San Francisco, and Washington, D.C. All of these were now gone, mostly for lack of funding.

Andrew believed that the principal loss from removing seminary representatives from the board, identified in the crisis laid out before this consultation ten years later, was the lack of ownership for the organization and the program by its membership — which clearly affected student enrollment. Was it possible to have both independence and investment from consortium member schools?

*   *   *

The present board of directors, Andrew thought, was in about the same place he was at this point — undecided about SCUPE's future. The divergent viewpoints expressed in the three consultations raised important issues and interesting ideas, but not did not result in new investment by member seminaries. In fact, the consortium members had voted to cut their fees by more than half. SCUPE's declining enrollment, correspondingly weak financial condition, and consequent downsizing of staff were all depressing trends; Andrew did not expect any significant help from the seminaries around whose needs SCUPE had been built.

The current board members had all been attracted by SCUPE's strengths: its integration of study, action, and theological and personal reflection; its biblical grounding and consideration of the strengths of different theological camps; its systematic understanding of the city and holistic vision of ministry; its theological focus on the principalities and powers active in the city and the church's prophetic mission to them; its network of peers and supporters engaged in ministry, who respected SCUPE's long-standing commitments and quality programs. While board members were clearly concerned about SCUPE's present condition and its future, they continued to invest their time and support because they believed in what the organization was about.

What should he bring to the board next week? Should SCUPE plan to shut down entirely? It might be the option most fair to staff facing late paychecks, years on end without cost-of-living raises, and a future that could only be a gamble.

Andrew put a disk in his computer and began drafting his report and recommendations to the board:

> SCUPE is faced with significant opportunities for new program development and at the same time serious questions of governance and finance. . . .

Background: Whose Program Is It?
Seminary Consortium for Urban Pastoral Education

The Seminary Consortium for Urban Pastoral Education (SCUPE) was founded in 1976 in Chicago by six theological seminaries. SCUPE's mission statement is to "develop leaders and provide consultation and educational resources for individuals, educational institutions, churches and agencies that seek to enhance the spiritual, social, and physical quality of life for those who live in the city." At the time of the case, SCUPE offered two programs in keeping with this mission: a nine-month internship program designed for seminary students and the Congress on Urban Ministry, a networking, training, and worship resource for those engaged in or wishing to learn about urban ministry. This conference brought together in Chicago several hundred urban practitioners, usually every two years.

The case takes place in the academic year 1996-97, when SCUPE held a series of three one-day consultations with representatives of member and non-member seminaries. Enrollment had declined over the prior decade from some 30 full-time students to 5 in 1995-96. This decline forced staff cuts, and SCUPE's board and director decided not to offer any programs in 1996-97 in order to focus on rebuilding and restructuring.

SCUPE sees itself existing in and between two primary contexts: that of the city and that of the seminary. The consortium relates to the city as a body of interrelated systems (political, economic, social, ecological), and as part of a metropolitan area. While promoting a holistic understanding of the metropolis, SCUPE board and staff also follow the biblical preferential option for the poor, giving particular attention to communities marginalized and oppressed by the powers at work in the city. Early in its history, SCUPE made analysis of urban systems a cornerstone of its curriculum. For the last decade this has been furthered theologically with an emphasis on the biblical understanding of "principalities and powers," drawing on the work of William Stringfellow and Walter Wink. SCUPE encourages students to see the structures and forces at work in the city, even the city itself, each as a power with a life and integrity of its own.

SCUPE sees poverty as an issue that presents one of the strongest challenges to churches and the city. More than an economic condition, poverty reflects dislocation (homelessness, the creation and destruction of public housing, and the abandonment and gentrification of various neighborhoods) and marginalization (the loss not only of jobs but of whole industries, the lodging of great numbers of the population in prison, the loss of the power to vote for those labeled felons, and new forms of segregation between the middle class and the poor in such diverse areas as computer literacy, Internet access, and participation in the stock market). A trio of closely related issues — connected to the impact of poverty — are those of drug and alcohol addiction, street gangs, and urban violence. On a very localized level, the proliferation of gangs reflects and perpetuates the decline of families as primary social entities and forces in urban neighborhoods. On a broader level, the empowerment of gangs builds on an economic savvy regarding regionalization — the interdependence of cities, suburbs, and exurbs — as they develop supply chains and sales forces throughout and beyond metropolitan areas. In internship placements, students not only analyze particular principalities theologically, they often work directly with people impacted by drugs, alcohol, and street violence.

To address the city's continuing struggle with the related issues of racism, multiculturalism, and ethnic transition in neighborhoods, SCUPE courses focus on racism and ethnicity to help students understand the dynamics of race and multiculturalism. A number of students engage in cross-cultural ministry in their internship placements. In addition, a theology course on Christology and Culture examines the role culture plays in understanding the identity of Jesus, and the Congress on Urban Ministry regularly includes workshops on subjects such as multicongregational and multilingual churches. Although it traditionally has had a majority of Anglo males in attendance, the Congress is known for its diversity. There are a good number of female and African-American representatives, and Congress participants include clergy and laity from a broad range of denominations as well as age and education levels.

Prior to the internship program's being suspended, with the exception of three permanent staff, the teaching staff were all part-time faculty with other engagements in the community — pastors, activists,

151

academics, and leaders of other community agencies. About one-third were women; all had at least a master's degree, and most had doctorates. About half were Anglo, one quarter African-American, the other quarter Latina/o or Asian-American.

SCUPE sought out faculty who shared a commitment to biblical faith, to justice, and to the city. The director looked for "gifted communicators who are comfortable with students, capable of challenging them, knowledgeable and informed by their own ministry experience as well as their formal education, and who ideally understand and share SCUPE's theological lens of the principalities and powers and our social lens of the metropolis as a system of systems." In terms of methodology, SCUPE worked from its beginning to build an educational program that was critical, contextual, and experiential, integrating theory and practice — one not just geographically in the city, but engaged with it and open to the lessons to be learned from the urban context. SCUPE understands program participants to be adult learners, responsible for developing and carrying out their own learning agenda. "We depreciate any codependent model of education, where all rests on the instructor's knowledge and the students' ignorance."

The consortium has two sets of partners, one of which is the member seminaries that choose to join the consortium. Each one designates a representative, who is invited to provide input in meetings such as the 1996-97 consultations and to meet with a SCUPE staff member who visits each school at least once a year. Member schools also have a voice through their SCUPE students who evaluate every class.

Another set of partners are SCUPE's peers in the city — churches and community agencies, which supply faculty, internship sites, and students, and are represented on SCUPE advisory committees for various programs. Some of these partners come to the consortium, and some are sought out because of their innovative and high-quality work. Many of these individuals serve multiple roles: they may lecture for SCUPE, hire one of the students after graduation, or invite SCUPE to lead training for their staff.

Discussion Notes: Whose Program Is It?

Teaching Goals for Collaboration and Confession

- To explore approaches for developing and sustaining ownership in urban programs.
- To examine the social, economic, and organizational factors that affect urban theological education programs and their constituency.
- To consider criteria for evaluating the viability of programs for urban theological education.
- To consider the role of mission statements and doctrinal statements in guiding educational institutions.

I. Many of the conversations with representatives of SCUPE's member and non-member seminaries highlight the theme of ownership.

1. What are some critical marks or signs of ownership in an institution or program?

2. What steps were taken initially by SCUPE's director and board to insure the partner schools' ownership of the program?

3. What shifts occurred in the context, including in the student body and in seminary education, since the inception of the SCUPE program?

4. How did the SCUPE board — and the executive director — respond to these shifts? Consider changes in board membership and in funding approaches.

5. If SCUPE is to continue its student education program, what approaches could be taken to ensure greater ownership? In what ways, for example, could the current program be revised to be

more compatible with programs of member seminaries? What rationale supports each of these proposals?

II. The SCUPE program is struggling with student enrollment at the time of this case.

1. What are the underlying reasons for the decline in enrollment? Consider in this discussion the social and economic changes in the urban context, changes in the member schools and their student bodies, and changes in SCUPE.

2. Should enrollment be a "marker" of success? Why or why not?

3. What student body is served by SCUPE at the time of the case?

4. As Andrew Niemann struggles with dwindling numbers, what alternatives would you suggest for him and the board?

5. What programs or structural changes would be necessary to shift to a different constituency? What are the practical implications of such a shift? What is the theological rationale for suggested changes? How would SCUPE's mission change if its constituency changes?

   Consider asking small groups to discuss this last set of questions and each present a concrete scenario to the full group for further discussion.

III. At the close of the case, Andrew Niemann is seriously considering whether or not SCUPE should continue as an educational institution. What criteria should guide this decision? Consider SCUPE's primary assets. What are its liabilities? Advise Andrew on his presentation to the board and how he should structure the meeting.

IV. Andrew Niemann, as the founding executive director of SCUPE, recalled that early in SCUPE's formation, the board attempted to structure a doctrinal statement, but because of the mixture of theological perspectives represented among them, representatives of the founding schools decided to develop a mission statement instead.

1. Briefly glean from the case clues about the different theological perspectives of those whom Niemann interviews.

2. In the context of a theologically diverse constituency, what are some of the dangers of developing statements of doctrine that purport to speak for the whole organization?

3. What are the values of a doctrinal or confessional statement for a faith-based organization?

4. On what biblical and theological tenets would you base SCUPE's ministry?

5. If you had been on the SCUPE board, would you have recommended that SCUPE create a doctrinal or confessional statement? Why or why not? How might having a doctrinal statement affect SCUPE's ministry?

Case Study: A Metro Strategy

"Father John, shall I unlock the church for the Parish Council meeting?" asked James Reynolds, the Council chair.

"Please do, James. Security is a real issue at St. Mary's these days," replied parish priest John O'Sullivan. Father John knew his lay leaders were expecting his recommendation on whether or not to join several other congregations in the Metro Strategy training program for urban ministry. Despite a week of prayer and struggle following a presentation about the program to the Parish Council, he was still undecided whether joining Metro Strategy would be an opportunity or a disaster.

St. Mary's Catholic Church served 2,000 families on the edge of Los Angeles's poorest region, South Central. The congregation included a few white families, mostly retired, who had lived in the parish since the 1940s. African Americans, such as the Council chair, were now the largest active ethnic group in the parish. A small but faithful Filipino immigrant contingent was also present in the congregation. By the 1990s South Central had a majority Latino population, as did St. Mary's parish. However, only those Latinos who were comfortably bilingual were active in the congregation. Although there was one weekly mass in Spanish by a visiting priest, all the other masses were in English.

This case was written by Robert A. Evans and Alice Frazer Evans. Copyright © 1999, The Case Study Institute. All names have been disguised to protect the privacy of the individuals involved in this situation.

Father John was assigned as the parish priest five years ago at the age of 50. He lost his associate pastor two years ago due to the shortage of priests in the archdiocese. The English masses were well attended, and finances were adequate despite rapidly growing poverty in this part of the city. Demands for the liturgical and educational services of the parish were high. St. Mary's was viewed in the diocese as a solid congregation still holding its own in a transitional neighborhood.

Father John invited a colleague, Father Michael Ryan, and a team from his parish to make a presentation to St. Mary's Council after hearing him speak about Metro Strategy at an area meeting of priests. Father John thought the program would get more laity involved in the life of the congregation. He also thought community organizing might help address some of the growing social problems of the area. He knew that the Industrial Areas Foundation had worked with many of the congregations now involved in Metro Strategy. They had trained clergy and lay leaders to take action on social issues that affected their communities. IAF campaigns had addressed issues such as affordable housing, alternatives to gang violence, public school accountability, citizenship training, and raising California's minimum wage.

While he worried about IAF's activist, confrontational style, John understood from Michael that Metro Strategy was developing a theology of urban action and a new approach to capacity building among congregational leaders. Metro Strategy was based solidly on Christian and democratic values. Its goal was to build a relational culture to transform neighborhoods in one of the poorest but also one of the most ethnically and culturally diverse parishes in the city.

The previous week, Father Michael had begun the presentation to the Parish Council with a study of Luke 4:14-21, focusing on Jesus' mission to proclaim good news to the poor. He then asked members of St. Mary's Council, "What kind of parish do you have and what kind of parish do you want?" Council members looked uneasy at first, but soon began to respond openly: "We have a good parish." "We meet the needs of our members." "We offer masses at convenient times." "We provide fine catechism training." "We support our youth." "We offer baptism and anointing." Chairman James Reynolds seemed to summarize their views as he said, "At St. Mary's we serve the people and build up the parish and our faith."

Father Michael proceeded,

You can be not just a *good* parish, but an *excellent* parish. As we know, it was not Christ's intention to build himself up but rather to build the Kingdom of God. Is the role of the church to build itself up — or to build the Kingdom of God? The vision of the church in Metro Strategy has three implications. First is evangelization that reaches out beyond our normal parishioners to those who need the love and care of the church. Second is a new leadership role for lay people, not to take over the tasks of the priest, but rather to give leadership in their community as a consequence of their baptism. This is a leadership to change and transform the city in the vision that Christ had for the Kingdom of God. Third, like Jesus, we are called to pronounce good news to the poor and to work for justice in everything that we do in our community as well as in our parish.

Father John recalled how Lydia Muñoz, the Hispanic woman on the team, shared her story with the Council. "I grew up in Ecuador with a traditional upbringing in the church. When my husband, daughter, and I moved to Los Angeles, we were invited by lay leaders of our parish to come to church." Lydia then reflected on her journey:

The real challenge to me was becoming aware of my role in the world. Community action was never encouraged in my home parish. Through the IAF training, I learned about the injustices endured by members of our parish and neighborhood. I was particularly concerned about those called "illegal immigrants," and I was deeply hurt by those people who supported California Proposition 187. This bill — which would prevent illegal immigrants and their children from receiving social services — divided us into first- and second-class people and promised to deprive many Spanish-speaking people of their rights to education and health care. I joined demonstrations to protest this bill. I also learned about evaluating our community and about my own rights and power as a citizen. The church helped me to be an actor in changing my community — not a victim. I had often worked as an altar server and as a choir member, but I now see my service as a Christian is also to work for justice and to serve those who are not members of my congregation. Teaching a citizenship class in the evening is part of my ministry.

Norman Jones, another member of the team, shared his perspective:

> I am concerned with the way California is polarized by debates on issues such as Proposition 187. People begin to distrust each other and strengthen their negative stereotypes about those from particular ethnic traditions, especially Hispanics. This makes marginal people even more vulnerable and powerless. Metro Strategy helps people in our congregations develop personal and relational power so we can work together as change agents. Only when we act collaboratively can we get access to decent health care, education, or unemployment and retirement benefits. It's not enough simply to be a citizen or a voter when some of our neighbors have to work two or three jobs just to keep their families alive. To have an excellent parish means that lay leaders make a difference not only in our congregations but also in our communities. This is what the Kingdom of God is about. Most important for me is that I am learning to draw on my faith for meaning. Spirituality is sometimes seen as private or individual devotion, but I discovered it has even greater power when it bonds me to God and other people.

When asked about the specific design for the program, Father Michael identified several steps. Father John and the Council would identify 20 to 30 people in the parish who were not on the Council. Team members would interview each one and select 10 leaders to form St. Mary's strategy team. These 10 would meet for a year with the larger multicultural, multi-denominational group for Bible study and training. The course would include study of Exodus and the meaning of Covenant; study of theology including the meaning of the Body of Christ and the role of the church in the world; social and political analysis; and sharing personal experiences about what participants' faith said about the economy, family, ecology, or the role of the church. They would learn skills such as how to conduct house meetings to analyze local situations and how to identify new leaders. This group would then select an additional 10 leaders in their parish for training, and begin to think about where they want the parish to go, how they want catechism to be taught, or how they will build relationships between the parish and the community. Each member congregation has a representative on the Metro Strategy Board and pays dues, based on the congregation's income, to support the skilled community trainers provided by IAF.

Father Michael then asked St. Mary's Parish Council members for their questions and reflections.

James Reynolds, the Chairman of the Parish Council, responded, "I would love to develop a wider group of strong leaders in our parish. The fifteen members of our Council are exhausted by trying to assist Father John with the work of the Parish. If this training produces stronger parish leaders, I support it."

Raul Marcos, the only Filipino member of the Council, responded hesitantly, "We could use more leaders in this parish, but I am not sure if what your team describes is the kind of leadership we need. The kind of activism you see may be fine if you are at the heart of South Central, but most of our parishioners are not likely to become involved in demonstrations at the INS offices or before the City Council. It sounds like the kind of activism I experienced in the Philippines that split the church wide open. People became more concerned about their political positions than their faith, and the church became a threat to the local and national government agencies. Rather than being agents of reconciliation in their communities, some churches became agents of confrontation. I came to the United States to get away from conflicts in the Philippines."

Robert Hill, one of the many African Americans on the Parish Council, reflected, "I would really like to learn how we connect our faith with our lives. We do a lot of talking about Jesus' love and compassion and service, but it is not always clear to me how that affects me at my work at a construction company that is struggling to survive. If this training could help us understand how to be effective Christians, in our community as well as our congregations, I think it would be a great gift. The question is, do we have enough people in our parish who are willing to take the training and risk speaking out for justice? We are a pretty comfortable parish at the moment; I'm not sure we feel the hurt in our part of the city strongly enough to risk our comfort."

Carolyn Brown, another African American on the Council, added, "I am a mother of two teenagers. What worries me is how we keep our young people related to the church. We want our children to serve as acolytes and be active in the choir and youth group. Their moral values

160

are constantly under threat in this city, and we have to protect them. They need examples of mothers and fathers who are regularly at mass, frequently in prayer, and who are committed to sacrifice for the sake of their congregation. We must think about what we model for our children if we want them to be successful and responsible adults."

Janice Ray responded, "But most of our young people drop out when they are old enough to have a choice. They may be here at mass or doing youth work, but they are also wandering the streets rather than getting a good education. Conditions in our local schools are appalling, and our children are being drawn into the growing gang culture. Our children don't know whether they will have even as good jobs as we have. We need to be trained to bring about change, not for our sake but for the sake of our children. This is the kind of modeling they need."

"Who would be our partners in this Metro Strategy? I understand you have not just Catholics, but Protestants and even unions and some parents' groups." William Ashby said this as he turned his chair toward the other members of the Parish Council and away from the team making the presentation. "I'm a factory manager, and I get nothing but grief from the unions. I think we have to be careful about who we collaborate with and what kind of partners the church has."

Malcolm Evers shook his head and looked at members of the visiting team. "We have to confess that we don't know how to get our people involved either in the life of the congregation or the life of the community. If this program offers a solid educational program for leaders, we need to take advantage of the opportunity. The days are gone when we should expect our priest to do everything. We must shoulder more of the responsibility for the work and life of this parish and try to make it a real community."

Fred Andrews, the oldest member of the Council, had been sitting quietly at the edge of the table and spoke softly, "I don't think we need to be organized. We have people teaching catechisms, serving on all the committees of the church, working for our feast days, and being involved in mission through our gifts. We support the local soup kitchen, we make our gifts to the archdiocese, and I think we are pretty well organized to serve our parish. I think it is a mistake to panic because the neighborhood is beginning to change. Our parish members have little in common with the new immigrants moving in. We can't suddenly focus on learning Spanish or changing our liturgies in order to respond to Mexicans who are taking our jobs, using our public services, and sending the money home to their families in Mexico. These will not be stable, permanent members of St. Mary's ten years from now. They will have moved on to another location. Let's not get over-organized."

James Reynolds, the Council chair, turned to his priest. "Father John, you have been unusually quiet tonight. What do you think about this urban strategy program?"

Father John recalled urging the members of the Council to be in prayer about the vision and the options they had heard about in the presentation. He appreciated the honest discussion of what kind of leadership the church needed in a changing society and neighborhood. He reminded them that they were a strong parish, and that they needed to make a choice about the programs they were involved in out of the strengths they had in the parish. Father John went on to promise that when the Parish Council met next week for a special meeting, he would respond to James's questions after he and the Council members had an opportunity to pray and think about it more. He thanked the visiting team for their presentation and closed the meeting with prayer.

Throughout the following week, Father John considered his conflicting views of the Metro Strategy invitation. He would love to have the capacity of his leaders developed to more effectively address challenges in the parish and the community. The problems of the neighborhood were enormous and growing: poverty, poor education, the rights of immigrants, equal access to economic opportunities, and the threat of crime and violence. These were overwhelming problems, and he was unsure whether his small parish and his lay leaders could make a difference in the city. While the Church had strong social teaching, Church leaders seldom offered concrete ways to address the issues.

Father John realized that his diocesan seminary education had given him classical academic preparation for saying mass, hearing confession, and anointing. Thirty years ago the seminary had not offered any understanding of the church as a catalyst in the community or enabled him to think of, much less train, parish leaders doing anything beyond assisting the priest. The training offered by Metro Strategy would not only build his own skills but his ability to support laity in addressing issues that directly affected the parish. In addition, there were already more than twenty congregations in the Metro Strategy project. The partnership with other pastors and community organizations could be exciting.

The kind of model that Father Michael was developing in his congregation was a significant paradigm shift in how ministry could be done in both Catholic and Protestant parishes. Father John was unsure he could handle a new ecclesiology that focused on lay rather than clergy leadership. He wanted and needed more lay leaders in the parish. But Father John suspected that the kind of training they would get in this program would focus on leadership in the community, not in the congregation. He would probably have less help, not more, in his priestly tasks if this approach were successful.

The priest thought about St. Mary's congregation. He agreed with Raul Marcos that programs focusing on social change often divided congregations as well as communities. Many of his faithful but conservative parishioners would certainly be disrupted and agitated by joining this program. The parish was doing pretty well. Maybe he would be able to get a Spanish-speaking associate who could help creatively address the parish transition without being involved in a more radical project like the Metro Strategy. Father Michael was doing great work in his parish, but that form of ministry may not be right for St. Mary's.

Father John slowly reread Luke 4, which begins with Christ's temptation in the wilderness. Were his fear of change and the relative comfort of his parish like the devil, trying to blind him and some of his parishioners to Christ's prophetic message of good news to the poor? He recalled Father Michael's challenge at the priests' meeting: "Priests should be keepers of the vision — not just keepers of the tradition."

For better or worse, Father John knew that his lay leaders looked to him for guidance. He was unsure what to say and how to say it. What he recommended would be influential in the decision that the parish made, not only about the Metro Strategy, but also about the future of the congregation. He heard the lay leaders greeting one another in the next room, and he knew the meeting of the Parish Council was about to begin.

Background: A Metro Strategy
Industrial Areas Foundation — Metro Strategy

The Industrial Areas Foundation (IAF), which originated in Chicago, began organizing in inner-city Los Angeles in 1975 with pastors from different denominations who ministered in predominantly African-American and Latino congregations. One of the areas that became most active was South Central Los Angeles.

During the past fifty years, hundreds of thousands of African-American families moved to South Central, where they established a social and political base. In the late 1980s and 1990s many upwardly mobile youth and financially stable older African Americans chose to move from the area, leaving behind many poor and elderly. In the past fifteen years, South Central has received tens of thousands of Spanish-speaking immigrants from Central America. Many from rural Mexico lack literacy and job skills. Also in the past fifteen years, more than 100,000 middle-income jobs were lost in South Central, leaving primarily minimum-wage jobs. About 60 percent of the population has no health insurance. Other problems identified by local clergy and residents are: overcrowding; substandard dwellings; the inability of the public school system to adequately educate a large new diverse population; and a cultural "disconnect" between immigrant parents and their children, who reject their parents' culture but are lost to their own cultural identity. About 50,000 poor Latino immigrant families and African Americans worship in South Central churches on Sundays. A faith-based congregation is the only mediating institution for most of these residents.

The primary mission of IAF is to develop the capacity of congregational leaders to take action on issues that affect their families and their community. Based on the Judeo-Christian call to be agents of change within the world, IAF multi-denominational and multi-ethnic member congregations make a covenant with each other to use their combined capacity and power to confront and change the large-scale institutions, businesses, and political systems that negatively affect the lives of their families. Leadership training workshops expose faith-based congregations, unions, and other organizations to a continuous, repeated cycle of training, action, and evaluation. Some of the actions in which IAF congregations have been involved are:

- An organized campaign to raise the minimum wage in California.
- Nehemiah West, a campaign to build 400 family-owned afford-able houses in Compton and Bell Gardens, poor cities adjacent to South Central.
- Hope in Youth, a five-year campaign in Los Angeles County to give youth alternatives to gang violence.
- Kids First, a campaign to hold public schools accountable for ed-ucation.
- Active Citizenship Campaign, a four-year program in which 32,000 new U.S. citizens living in Los Angeles learned skills of citi-zenship, community responsibility, leadership, and public action.

A critical turning point for IAF came in the 1990s when the state voted overwhelmingly in favor of Proposition 187, which made it illegal to use state funds to provide education and health care to children of undocumented immigrants. Church leaders and most faith-based in-stitutions had made strong public statements against this "repressive and unjust law." Nevertheless, large numbers of Catholics and Protes-tants voted with the majority of the state in favor of the bill. Church leaders realized the church had lost its ability to influence the moral choices of its own members.

While IAF leaders knew the organization had achieved significant political victories in the past, they felt they were not building suffi-ciently powerful coalitions to bring about systemic change in society. Several leaders decided to focus on an "alliance for change," which they titled Metro Strategy. Their goal was to:

- Develop a relational culture within congregations.
- Knit multi-ethnic and multi-denominational congregations into covenant partners.
- Develop the capacity of congregational leaders to transform their congregations and society.
- Develop the theology of this work out of the Judeo-Christian tra-dition.

The theology of Metro Strategy was based on Judeo-Christian assumptions that "each person is created in the image and likeness of God, and that the human person develops that capacity to be fully human in relationship to others." "Because we are all members of one Body, we have a shared life. Therefore when one person is damaged or diminished, then the whole Body suffers. Therefore we are called to the work of enhancing all members of our society in their capacity to exercise their own gifts and abilities in relationship with others so that the Body of Christ is built up."

Metro Strategy, which does not provide either a degree or a certificate, offers a ten-day training for pastors and lay leaders. Staff members subsequently mentor participants "so that they are stretched to achieve their full ability." Metro Strategy courses focus on developing "relational power" and helping people move from being overwhelmed to transforming those situations of oppression in which they live. Faculty and participants read theology, political analysis, and social philosophy and engage each other in reflection from local and personal experience. Faculty members find that the most effective teaching approach to prepare leaders for urban ministry is a constant cycle of analysis, action, and reflection. Participants craft their own stories and learn how to do "one-on-ones" where they search for leaders and not victims. They conduct house meetings to do analysis of local situations within the larger urban context. They learn how to go into action and how to value their own story and see its significance in the larger society. All of the courses and programs deal with the relationship between participants' faith and their work, family, and public institutions. The training is always done in a multiethnic and ecumenical or interfaith context.

The Metro Strategy approach to multicultural reality is to help people move beyond the politics of racial identity to explore the new reality that can be created by collaboration. Facilitators conduct conflict transformation workshops to develop skills in conflict mediation and transformation. The basic goal is for the African-American and the Latino populations to be able to ask one another, "How can we work together to respond to your needs and mine?" In working with clergy and laity, staff members feel that the greatest service urban pastors can perform for their congregations is to "move beyond preoccupation with survival and administration" and to help lay members "develop their own power and their own capacity."

Metro Strategy employs Industrial Area Foundation organizers as faculty for the Metro Strategy project. The ten-member full-time faculty includes four women and six men from the Los Angeles metropolitan area. One is Japanese, four are Latino, one African American, and four Anglo. One is an Episcopal priest. All are degreed and are experienced community organizers. In addition, these organizers constantly seek to identify potential teachers and equip them to move into teaching roles.

At the time of the case, Metro Strategy had 60 partner organizations and a leadership body of 250 men and women from a broad variety of church groups — Roman Catholic, Lutheran, Episcopal, Jewish, and Presbyterian. This included a balanced combination of laity, clergy, African-American, Latino, Anglo, and Korean participants. Partner organizations were primarily congregations but also included parent/teacher organizations and some local unions. Each partner organization pays dues according to ability and has membership on the strategy board. In the next ten years Metro Strategy hopes to expand its membership to include mediating institutions throughout Los Angeles County, with a goal of 500 congregations, unions, temples, mosques, and housing projects.

Discussion Notes: A Metro Strategy

Teaching Goals on Collaboration and Confession

- To explore the theological implications of the role and mission of the church, particularly for local congregations equipping their members for urban ministry.
- To consider the implications of adapting traditional models of community organizing (collaboration) to parish- and faith-based (confession) models of education and action such as Metro Strategy.
- To consider the pastoral and educational challenges inherent in dealing with diverse, often conflicting views of church members.
- To engage participants in sharing their own theological perspectives on urban ministry.

Discussion Approach

I. Context

1. Focus the discussion by reading aloud Luke 4:14-21.

2. Have participants clarify

> —the social and economic context of South Central Los Angeles;
> —the specific context of St. Mary's Church.

II. Issues

1. Identify the goals of the Metro Strategy program. Explore more deeply the collaborative, confessional, and spiritual dimensions of the program.

What are the advantages and disadvantages of an ecumenical approach?

What are the implicit and explicit understandings of the mission of the Church for Metro Strategy?

2. What understandings of the mission of the Church emerge in St. Mary's Council? What experiential, confessional, and spiritual sources inform these understandings?

III. Alternatives

1. Father John is being pushed by the Church Council for his response. Divide participants into small groups of five to six people. Each group is to develop three to four specific strategies (or guiding principles) that they advise Father John to follow to enable the Council to make a decision about Metro Strategy. Post these on newsprint for general discussion. Conclude this session with a discussion of what participants learned from one another. Discuss the effects of collaboration on the decision-making process.

2. An alternative approach for this section is to build a "group" role-play with the participants counseling Father John, played by the facilitator or one of the participants. "Father John" should push his counselors for their reasons why Metro Strategy would be good for St. Mary's why it would not be good for the parish.

   Close this session by asking participants what understanding of the mission of the church informed their suggestions to Father John and the council. On which scriptural or confessional resources did they draw for their advice?

IV. Additional Topics and Questions for Discussion

The following questions are adaptable to a variety of discussion goals and groups.

1. What are the most effective and faithful strategies to fulfill the church's mission in the city?

> The Industrial Areas Foundation is known in many areas of the U.S., including Los Angeles, for aggressive community organizing that has not always been related to the church. What are the advantages and disadvantages for Metro Strategy of the close connection with this program? What theological questions are raised by aggressive community-organizing strategies?

> What is meant by "evangelism in the city"?

> How is evangelism related to issues of justice?

> What are the advantages and disadvantages of an ecumenical approach?

> What is meant by a holistic urban strategy for ministry?

2. Why (or why not) is collaboration needed in the city? What are the challenges of collaborative efforts in urban ministry?

3. How do you understand spirituality in an urban setting? (For example, personal, social, civic.) What are the challenges in terms of spirituality for Christians who feel called to work for justice?

4. Luke 4:14-21 is cited by Father Michael as the biblical standard for parish life. Do you agree? Why or why not? What other biblical passages are appropriate standards? Why?

5. According to Father Michael, Jesus' role is "building up the Kingdom of God," not himself, the church, or — by implication — the local parish. What impact does this interpretation have for setting priorities for urban ministry?

6. Many urban youth are leaving the church and are in trouble in the streets. How would a new theological paradigm for urban ministry transform the church to address the concerns of and about young people?

7. The Metro Strategy proposes a vision for the role of lay people in the community. Theologically and practically what are the implications of this vision for the relationship between clergy and laity?

8. To what extent should the context affect the content of theological education for urban ministry? Discuss this question as it relates to the specific context of South Central Los Angeles and to theological education in general. In your experience, what currently determines the curriculum and content for theological education?

9. Father John acknowledges that his classical, academic theological studies did not adequately prepare him for urban ministry. What changes can or should be made in the ministerial preparation of clergy and lay leaders for urban ministry?

Commentary

WARREN L. DENNIS

This commentary seeks not to be simply one more academic conversation about urban ministry. It will reflect the post–World War II development of the urban ministry movements that have sought to be more collaborative and confessional while at the same time attempting to change pedagogical practices in seminaries, churches, and communities. Building on this pedagogical history of urban ministry, my aim is to discern in the two cases the emerging curricula for community-based spiritual formation and public participation by theological education programs.

I am particularly interested in the theological reality of the empowerment of persons victimized by systemic oppression and violence to speak to the realized presence of God's affirming acts in their lives. They are willing to collaborate with the academy and the church on common missiological concerns and have put into practice the spiritual teachings of the community.

What makes the SCUPE and Metro Strategy programs so confessional is their commitment to follow the living Lord into the desolate places of inner-city life. Each program has a deep commitment for doing justice in places where justice is rare. Both approaches to urban ministry challenge participants to raise the model of Christ in the midst of conflict, uncertainty, and timidity. These programs call us to move beyond the safe confines of the walls of the church and academy and to speak a prophetic word to those in power who sometimes do irreparable harm to defenseless women and children who call the inner city home.

The two strategies for urban ministry represent a sense of spiritual discernment and analysis of public policy and the resulting collaboration among individuals and institutions. They challenge the way we think about faith and action in the public arena where theological reflection is a minor player in matters of public discourse. Both cases

172

conclude with the underlying question: Where do we go from here? The inherent question is: What are the theological mandates that undergird their program? What is at stake here, however, is far more than Director John Andrew's view of SCUPE reinventing itself, or what Father John O'Sullivan of St. Mary's Roman Catholic Church will say or not say to his parish council about joining the Metro Strategy leadership training for urban ministry.

The central urban ministry premise I wish to explore in this commentary is the need to bridge the gulf between learning, faith, and practice by implementing faith commitments through public policy in the academy, church, and community. Across the North American theological enterprise, a conversation is taking place about faith and public participation. The dialogue is about teaching and learning, curricula development, credentialing, and the economic well-being of the community. In some cases, the conversation is within seminaries around the classical argument of theology and practices. In other instances, the conversation is an interdenominational and interfaith postmodern discussion focused on expanding urban theological education beyond the traditional boundaries to discern the best content and teaching practices for urban ministry. Urban ministry advocates in this conversation challenge seminaries to assume greater public responsibility for helping urban congregations and other private and not-for-profit institutions shape the character of effective urban ministry for this new century. In order to do so, seminaries require critical thinking, constructive ideas, collaborative models, and courage. The question asked is: How do we learn from the communities where we are located? Local congregations, such as in the Metro Strategy case study, may spearhead the conversation.

The Metro Strategy case invites us to become participant-observers as the parish council discusses the pros and cons of joining other congregations in a training program for urban ministry. SCUPE's consultants allow us to witness the tension between a commitment to take the gospel message of God's love and saving grace to the city and the struggle to survive amidst curricula change, demographic shift in the student population, and decline in seminary participation in urban programs. Changes for both institutions are accompanied by population shifts over the last thirty years that intensify both class and race division. The power of classism and racism must be grappled with in considering the larger context of urban life. In light of these historical, social, and theological changes, urban theological education must become more transparent and more self-critical. We must look rigorously at its teaching and learning methods, especially in terms of confessional or spiritual development and leadership formation. A period of change also provides an opportunity for IAF–Metro Strategy and SCUPE to exemplify their potential for institutional collaboration.

My personal involvement with such programs goes back thirty years to my experience as a trainee in the Action Training Movement of which SCUPE is an outgrowth. During this time I witnessed the importance of academy, church, and grassroots collaboration on issues of racial reconciliation and community empowerment through leadership development. I saw firsthand the significant contribution made by dedicated clergy persons who saw the city as their calling. These men and women stood on the margins of the institutional church and modeled for me a ministry of teaching and learning that is the foundation for much that is espoused in urban ministry today. The Action Training Movement — or church-based urban training — encouraged direct engagement in and systematic reflection on the inner workings of the social, political, and economic systems that shape the policies that work against a community's best interests. The paradigm shift of the Action Training Movement was the emphasis on contextual analysis and the inclusion of racial ethnic concerns as integral to theological reflection on issues of ministry and mission. It attempted to establish a knowledge base that furthered the exploration of systemic analysis and reflection as forms of instruction.

Cincinnati's Community Human and Action Resource Training, CHART, in conjunction with the Community Planning Department of the University of Cincinnati, played a significant role in my formation and adherence to the philosophy of the Action Training Movement. CHART emphasized the importance of building community from the inside out. Being a part of this unique urban training program, whose purpose was to train teams of local citizens for planned community change, taught me the importance of cooperative theological education where the community is the pedagogical center. It is in this light that I offer this commentary.

The Distinctive Ministry of SCUPE

SCUPE faces a critical turning point in its long and marvelous history. Is SCUPE willing to be significantly different from what it once was, does it continue in the mode of decision-making within the limits of its original resources, or should it adapt to the present set of circumstances by developing one more program just to stay alive? It no longer has to be everything in urban ministry to everybody. On the other hand, does SCUPE attempt to reinvent itself by becoming smaller and more portable, or does it celebrate its accomplishments, close its doors for one last time, and fade into urban history having made a critical contribution? Rather than a disaster, closing may be an affirmation worthy of a glorious celebration.

SCUPE's strength as a consortium is its confessional affirmation of a missional theology to improve the spiritual, social, and physical qualities of life for those living in the city. This theology is informed by a preferential option for the poor and, through a curriculum of spiritual discernment, a commitment to encourage students to see the Word of God at work in the structures and forces in the city. SCUPE distinguishes itself by a commitment to work with the poor, to be with them in their struggle for justice, and to give systematic attention and guidance to communities that are marginalized and oppressed. SCUPE's curriculum acknowledges systemic evil as a premise that underscores the importance of ecumenical dialogue about the best ministry practices for addressing the ills of the city and the celebration of religious diversity in urban ministry. It has brought thousands of clergy, lay, and grassroots persons together biannually for the last twenty years to network and share approaches to urban issues. In brief, SCUPE's effectiveness is its ecumenical approach based on: (1) a relational principle whose purpose is from the bottom up — that affirms the dignity of all people; (2) its teaching, which is "narrow and deep" in scope because bigger is not necessarily better; and (3) its ability to enfold its ecumenical constituency into a supportive community that has a spiritual foundation.

Anthony Hutchinson, dean of a SCUPE member seminary, is partly right when he says: "It is important that we understand this is the late nineties, not the late sixties." Implicit in his statement is the assumption that "urban" is not only arguably an illusive term but it is no longer a priority since we live in a suburban-dominated ministry context. He is partly right. We live in a majority white middle-class society whose political mind-set is suburban. However, we find ourselves challenged daily by the encroachment of urban phenomena. The debate over the definition of urban is a political distraction that keeps us from focusing on the real problems of the inner city. Beyond simply signifying a population threshold, "urban" suggests an environment that is multicultural, multilinguistic, multiracial, and economically diverse. I am amazed that a debate continues in the midst of such blurred urban-suburban boundaries. More than ever before, we are embarking on a new urban reality that expands the definition of urban to encompass a metro-urban character. This metropolitan character of the merger of suburban-urban public policy, population, commerce, information technology, land-use, and governance calls for new curricula responses to preparation for urban ministry. This means that urban ministry in the twenty-first century must recognize the urban-suburban dichotomy, and that programs like SCUPE have to be more sophisticated in collaborating and organizing around matters of justice and equality.

A Metro Strategy of Collaboration

Both SCUPE and Metro Strategy challenge us to rethink our understanding of ecumenicity and the "place" of theological inquiry. With whom do we collaborate and where do we gather? This is a whole new way of conceiving and talking about curricula outside the academy and the doors of the church. If the goal is preparing students, clergy, and lay leaders for a twenty-first-century urban ministry, if this ministry must lead to spiritual and literal collaboration with grassroots communities to bring about significant change for a better quality of life, then the urban church and the theological academy must come to see *the city as text*. What is implied here is collaborative pedagogical method or what I refer to as interdisciplinary teaching.

In urban ministry, interdisciplinary analysis involves theological dialogue with non-faith-based disciplines or sciences: civil and criminal justice, sociology, business, medicine, education, anthropology, psychology, and so forth. The aspirations of the broad spectrum of constituencies, institutions, and individuals that comprise the city become the classroom where ministry is learned. In essence, the seminaries must be able to discern God's self-disclosure and self-revelation in the lives of the people, whether or not they are members of the church. "The church," says Cecil Williams, "is literally the extended family of humanity. It is not just believers. The church includes people who may not claim to be a part of the church, but they belong because they are part of the extended family of humanity."[1] In other words, the community systems, institutions, and people of the city must be engaged in the educational process as subject rather than as object.

The uniqueness of the Metro Strategy program is its collaborative method of teaching and learning beyond the traditional classroom. Rooted in the political, multiracial, church-based, community organizing philosophy of Saul Alinsky ("You never do for others what they can do for themselves"), founder of the Industrial Area Foundation in the back yards of Chicago in the 1940s, Metro Strategy members are willing to engage in direct action that is not a comfortable solution for all members of the parish council of St. Mary's. The key distinction of Alinsky's model was the use of confrontation and power as ingredients in every community transaction. Father Michael Ryan leads Father John O'Sullivan and members of his parish council in a conversation about the necessity for direct engagement and interdisciplinary reflection. Theology has the potential to become empowering and transforming when done in relationship to personal experiences of injustice.

Programs Based on Interdisciplinary Reflection

Congregations located in an urban context are not necessarily urban. In many instances, the members have mentally disconnected from the community, and in most cases they travel *in* to worship and leave with no intimate relationship with the neighborhood. They may not be in touch with the social, cultural, and spiritual life of the community. Some congregations physically located in an urban area have little notion of the prayers of the people. True urban congregations, however, are teaching and learning congregations. While worship is central,

1. Cecil Williams and Rebecca Laird, *No Hiding Place: Empowerment and Recovery for Our Troubled Communities* (San Francisco: HarperCollins, 1992), p. 22.

these congregations have an acute understanding of theological and ecclesiastical history, an appreciation of religious plurality, an awareness
of the evolution of urban land-use and public policy, and urban approaches to pastoral ministry. Inner-city congregations like St. Mary's
and theological education programs like SCUPE benefit from knowing
the historical intersections of faith and public life.

Programs like SCUPE and Metro Strategy must take caution not
to develop a "fix-it" type approach or develop programs "for the sake of
it" without doing the proper research, asking the root, causal questions, and taking into account a thorough understanding of the nature
of the situation or the underlining public policy implications. For instance, does it make a difference in the approach to a high-intensity
poverty neighborhood to have some knowledge about the impact of
poverty on the economic, social, and cultural characteristics of the
neighborhood? Saying *yes* is not enough. It is better to seek an interdisciplinary approach to urban ministry that involves spiritual discernment of the powers and principalities as well as a thorough knowledge
of urban phenomena. Then we may be more adequately equipped to
understand what constitutes the way the church should view ministry
in the city. This interdisciplinary knowledge might include, for example, the impact of health-care or education policy on the economic
transformation of an inner-city neighborhood. In his presentation, Father Michael is motivated by this broader view to say to the parish
council reflecting on Luke 4:14-21: "You can be not just a *good* parish,
but an *excellent* parish."

My interpretation of Luke 4:14-21 is that it is not a theology for
the well educated, affluent, and powerful. These verses are about the actual lives and struggles of poor people in their communities. "Faith," in
this instance, "is defined by one's solidarity with the poor expressed
most concretely by interacting in relations which presume that poor
people are the authorities on formulating the terms of their life conditions, and by participating in their religious expressions of resistance,
acceptance, and sanctification."[2] This means that urban theological education must engage in the kind of analysis that confronts the inter-
locking systems of oppression that prevent urban communities from

2. Elizabeth M. Bounds, Pamela K. Brubaker, and Mary E. Hobgood, eds.,
Welfare Policy: Feminist Critiques (Cleveland: Pilgrim Press, 1999), p. 69.

being whole, from being family. In other words, seminaries, urban churches, and the grassroots people must work in collaboration to be able to recognize the word of God in the world and the structures and forces working to create a just life.

Proclaiming the Gospel in the City

One of the greatest problems facing urban America is including the spiritual voice of marginalized faith communities in advancing the moral discourse in the public arena. There is a moral urgency for the seminary community, in partnership with congregational leaders and grassroots communities, to enter public debate of values that offset the common good. When communal values such as public safety, adequate health care, quality education, economic security, aesthetic surroundings, cultural identity, equality, and justice are not acknowledged, the seminary and the church should be prepared to demand their inclusion.

Luke 4:14-21 speaks to the social, political, and economic injustice faced by those on the "underside of history," who, upon reading it, may be transformed by its revolutionary precepts of the power of the "poor in history."[3] As the world becomes increasingly urbanized, persons proclaiming the gospel in the city must be knowledgeable about the systemic realities of urban life. They must be able to make connections between their faith and social change, be clear about individual and institutional responsibility to society, and respond with confidence to the gospel message of love and care of neighbor. It is in this context that the Metro Strategy case is significant.

Robert Hill of St. Mary's parish council reflects, "I would really like to learn how we connect our faith with our lives. . . . We are a pretty comfortable parish at the moment; I'm not sure we feel the hurt in our part of the city strongly enough to risk our comfort." His words present a ministry opportunity for the parish council as it struggles to move beyond its comfort zone into the community and assume greater lay leadership responsibility. He voices a profound ecclesiastical and col-

3. Gustavo Gutiérrez, *The Power of the Poor in History* (New York: Orbis Books, third printing, 1984), p. 171.

laborative challenge that is taking place in seminaries and urban congregations across the country as they re-evaluate the gospel message and the role of the church in the community.

According to the Metro Strategy for leadership training, the impetus for congregations to confess their commitment to follow Christ in the city in a new and fresh way should involve teaching and learning by listening to the community, participating in biblical study and reflection, and engaging in concrete civic action accompanied by theoretical inquiry. When people act, their action then affects the way they think. From this reflection and action paradigm come new forms of ministry and new ways of teaching. Metro Strategy is based on a theology of mission in which the gospel is inherently political while in practice it has specifically to do with pastoral care. The paradigm of listening, reflection, and action becomes actualized as the congregation and community become the learning modality for theological inquiry and interpretation. When such an approach is incorporated in the ecclesiology of the congregation, it challenges the people to make every effort to build communities of faith by learning from and working with grassroots people so that the church becomes woven into the fabric of the community.

Finally, urban ministry initiatives like Metro Strategy represent the next phase of urban theological education. However, they must themselves heed Father Michael's word of caution. Care should be taken by Metro Strategy leaders not to be just a good institute, but an excellent institute. The question, then, is what constitutes an excellent institute? A complete response awaits the development of a national criterion. However, we can make two important affirmations: *first,* that urban ministry done well celebrates the conscientization of a new heaven and new earth and, *second,* that congregations and their members are the primary bearers of the good news that draws diverse people into community and communion, where covenantal relation is proclaimed and claimed experientially. An excellent urban ministry institute thus serves as a provisional demonstration of the good news that, through the power of the Holy Spirit, our diversity contributes to the building up of community and the common good.

Commentary

MARY HENNESSEY, R.C.

The case study of the Seminary Consortium for Urban Pastoral Education (SCUPE) is deeply informed by the context of the era in which it was founded as well as the times through which it has survived. In the seventies, church judicatories and seminaries throughout the country were aware of their need to prepare ministers for a radically new urban environment that was dramatically changing the face of faith communities in the city. There was growing evidence that traditional seminary education was no longer sufficient for ministering in either the educated and consumption-driven suburbs or the uneasily shifting city, with the identifying cement of ethnic and cultural enclaves all but washed away.

At the same time, Christians were entering into new dialogue and openness with one another, learning how ignorant they were of one another, finding, in this period when there was so much fierce rage and polarization over the nation's politics and policies, that their convictions and beliefs might be more compatible with those of members of other denominations than with those of members of their own denomination. It was a time for collaboration, for working with others on common goals that could not, or were not, being met by individual churches alone. Within theological education this led to, among other things, consortia of theological schools and seminaries as well as joint ventures in training for urban ministry. Both religious conviction and perceived benefit generated much optimistic energy.

Working in such cooperative theological ventures taught me that if there is not a strong faith conviction regarding the importance and rightness of working together AND the awareness that, in working together, there will be benefits that could never be achieved singly, there will be an attrition of attention and involvement by the seminaries, most easily diagnosed when reduction in active board participation occurs. The cooperative venture may still exist on paper, its stationery may still be usable, but the platelet level in the programs and the projects will have dropped alarmingly. So when I learned that within a year of its inception, SCUPE's founding seminaries were beginning to distance themselves from responsibility for maintaining the urban training program, despite its proven effectiveness, I was more surprised that SCUPE had been able to continue the seminary program for some twenty years under these conditions than I was that this program was now in deep trouble. What a wonderful history: 400 students from 15 seminaries have participated in SCUPE's program, most of them for some nine months of solid experience in the city and careful political, sociological, and theological reflection and analysis upon the urban setting and ministry. This is an important contribution to the Christian community, one that the case indicates has been costly indeed for the SCUPE staff. We are all deeply in their debt.

This program gave SCUPE its name and identity. Now Andrew seems torn between investing more time and energy in it, and simply letting it go. SCUPE's staff evidences a grace-full openness to reading signs of the times. They had not waited for Dean Anthony Hutchinson to tell them that they are in the late nineties. Aware of the changes in urban church profiles and leadership, Lincoln Bradshaw and Kathleen O'Conner propose that SCUPE focus on educated and trained leadership for urban churches by way of a certification program. This would be designed to reach the many local pastors eager for education but not ready for a graduate degree program. This program would also reflect the shifts taking place in higher education as a whole, as older and part-time students become normative. Classes and faculty travel to where the students are: learning is becoming more accessible physically as well as psychologically. Classes and curriculum honor the multiple commitments typical of the adult learner. Look at any summer school brochure and see how the once common six-week courses have all but disappeared as one-week, two-week, and weekend courses proliferate, while throughout the year late-afternoon, evening, and Saturday courses are growing. Higher education generally finds that full-time graduate and undergraduate students now represent less than half of their student body.

Adult education experts agree that learning is more motivated and more effective when the adult learners are working at those things to which their study is related. Further enhancement comes when these students have a shared context for their work, as in the case of SCUPE's program. To teach local ministers in urban Chicago about the Chicago Housing Authority, for instance, would be immediately pertinent to all urban Chicago ministers, for the Chicago Housing Authority plays an important role in the provision and planning of low-cost housing throughout the city. When these adult learners bring their own experiences and analyses to the conversation, they become more fully partners in the learning experience, and learning is increased for everyone. More extensively than ever before, urban communities have the resources to call forth and develop their own leadership. The role of seminaries and educational programs may be called to change in order to provide these adult learners with an opportunity to shape their own education far more radically than in the past. At the same time, educational institutions have the power to validate these new ministerial leaders by the certificates and the degrees they confer, thus giving these leaders the educational credentials they sometimes need to open the doors in larger society's corridors of power.

If SCUPE were to move into a certification program for urban pastors or programs in community development, these could serve the city of Chicago well. How well would the member schools of the Seminary Consortium from which SCUPE derives its name see these programs as serving them? And how fully could SCUPE develop a certification program, given the ATS standards, if it wants to continue to provide accredited seminary training? The questions return to the issue of collaboration: Are the seminaries — and ATS — necessary partners for the theological education SCUPE wishes to offer? What religious convictions, what perceived benefits would guide the choices to be made?

Questions surrounding collaboration, determining who must be included, what will provide its warrant, and how it will be of benefit are also central to the second case study.

The Industrial Areas Foundation–Metro Strategy is deeply informed by its context. As early as the 1960s California experienced the impact of farm workers organized to successfully confront the growers and reach more equitable working conditions and wages. IAF programs developed in Southern California in 1981 against this background and upon principles drawn from the Judeo-Christian heritage. Through repeated cycles of training, action, and evaluation, IAF programs have helped the people of South Central Los Angeles to address issues such as the state's minimum wage, affordable housing, public education, and active and responsible citizenship. Now Father Michael, from a parish that belonged to IAF's Metro Strategy, has presented to Father John and his parish of St. Mary's the opportunity to join the Metro Strategy, thus becoming part of the network of churches with trained leaders working for the betterment of their very diverse and deprived urban area.

The goals of the Metro Strategy would seem to be self-evidently good for this community, situated in the midst of so many needs. The program surely affirms the commitment to social justice that the Roman Catholic Bishops of the U.S.A. had declared a "constitutive" dimension — not something that was optional or extra — of being a Catholic Christian. Yet in California at large, as economic conditions deteriorated in the state, Catholics and Protestants alike ignored the strong and vocal opposition of their church leaders and voted for legislation that so unjustly stripped the children of illegal immigrants of any public care that it was later overturned by the courts. It cannot be assumed, then, that this parish will automatically embrace this program.

Here again I would see their readiness to collaborate effectively and enduringly as depending upon both their "owned" faith convictions and a perception that Metro Strategy will bring genuine benefit. Metro Strategy's description of itself shows the desire to integrate and express its Judeo-Christian faith stance with the IAF strategies for change. In opening the meeting, Father Michael seems to want to communicate this. He begins with Scripture and then moves into a typical IAF question: "What kind of parish do you have and what kind of parish do you want?" He then moves on to present the implicit expectations of church in the Metro Strategy's vision: first, through evangelization, it will reach out to those who need the love and care of the church; second, it will support lay people, in response to their baptismal call, to take on leadership in expanding the reign of God in their community; and third, it will proclaim good news to the poor and work for justice.

When St. Mary's Parish Council members share their reflections and questions, it seems that, just as for SCUPE, either the religious conviction or the awareness of genuine benefit to themselves is not there.

184

"Activism divides," says a Filipino who evidently fled the experience of "people power" in the overthrow of Marcos. What is needed is that parents be good religious examples for their children, says an African-American mother, only to be refuted by another mother who wants the training in order to change her children's inadequate schooling. A factory manager asks if they can trust their potential partners in Metro Strategy since unions and parents' groups are included. Other voices, aware of the need to stimulate and train new lay leaders, have spoken in favor of Metro Strategy, but the eldest member of the Parish Council concludes the group's response by saying that there is no need to change: those who *really* belong are being cared for; those "others," who are Spanish speaking, taking "our" jobs, using "our" public services, sending money out of the country, will not be "stable, permanent members of St. Mary's ten years from now."

Father John's post-meeting ruminations reveal his own uncertainty and discomfort with this "new" theology that is fostering lay leadership and social justice, and they reveal his fear that the Metro Strategy would divide St. Mary's through its activism and drain away those who might help him in his "priestly tasks." Without religious conviction and with no sense of the benefit to the parish, how can Father John lead St. Mary's into successful Metro Strategy membership? While both the religious base and the IAF strategies were part of the meeting, I believe that there are some legitimate concerns if stronger connections are not made between the two. IAF has inherited the philosophy and strategy of Saul Alinsky, whose firm belief, so often stated, was that you had to have friction if you were going to have energy. Confrontation was essential because it created the friction; to increase the friction it was important to have a clearly defined "enemy" who was made to represent all that the people opposed. Alinsky believed that this confrontational power of those who came together out of self-interest was all that ordinary people had to oppose those with money and institutional power. Certainly this focused strategy brought results on specific issues. Certainly there have been adjustments in the training programs. What lingers is the language of "agitation" in the strategies of IAF and the issue of the long-term effect of the strategy on society and on those who shape the world in this way.

IAF seems to be rooted in an understanding of person that suggests that life is a relentless struggle in which energy must be generated to contain the self-interested push of any particular group to prevail excessively. Perhaps there is also a hint of Rousseau in its efforts to free those without societal power from society's oppression. (In fact, in some of IAF's ventures the leadership that IAF itself had forwarded eventually imitated the leadership it replaced.) Does power come from creating a critical mass that is driven by its own interests? I think we need to explore our theological understanding of the source of the power we seek to nourish. For me, it is intimately connected with the dignity of the person, not simply with a critical mass of bodies intent upon the same end. Many people advancing together can generate force, can overwhelm, but that is not the kind of power that is rooted in the Judeo-Christian tradition. For it is this kind of force that can act as though might makes right, that can lead to the tyranny of the majority. If we see human dignity as something bestowed by the Creator in an unconditional offer, as a gift that flows from God, and not as something that has come through human evolution, then we can move in a different way.

The importance of training is not to simply "empower," but to help us reach an awareness of God-given ability to respond to God's call to and gift of freedom. In this lies our dignity. The freedom to which God calls, the freedom that is God's gift, is the freedom that empowers us to choose how to respond within the realities of our lives, not negating what is there, but working with it, and accepting the responsibility to co-labor with God to bring about God's reign more fully. This is our first relationship and our first collaboration, but it cannot be separated from our relationship and collaboration with others because all that has been revealed to us of God through Jesus Christ tells us that authentic love — which is the most genuine relationship — of God, others, and self are inextricably intertwined. As IAF-Metro Strategy notes in its theological assumptions, "God is relationship."

All my work in urban ministry and urban theological education tells me that we can only reflect God's presence in the world when we are in relationship, choosing right relationships as fully as we can, welcoming the transformation that this makes possible in self, others, and society. The freedom that God bestows, that is the basis of our human dignity; it is the power to participate in shaping our world and ourselves in ways that most fully express the divine design, which is the fullness of shalom. To choose life is to choose to be free in this way, to have a horizon against which to examine both our goals and our techniques, and to have a commitment to be energized by linking with more co-laborers rather than targeting more enemies.

The profound theological assumptions of SCUPE are connected to these issues. SCUPE chooses to personify institutions, to give them a vocation and a call to exist. The discernment/analysis of institutions that this enables is powerful. This process of discernment/analysis is also appropriate for human persons, who for me have, because of divine creation, primary vocations from which are crafted the secondary vocations of institutions. An institution's right to exist is not absolute, and human persons can choose to end institutions; institutions have no right to end human persons. Institutions derive their vocations from the purpose they serve and are means for achieving something, while the dignity of the human person is God-given and can never be reduced to a means for something else.

Now, then, we can turn to the questions raised for SCUPE and for the Metro Strategy in their cases. Is SCUPE's seminary program fulfilling its vocation in the way that it currently collaborates with the seminaries and the city? My sense is that the relationship between them is not as right as it once was. The seminary representatives' comments at the meeting offer important pieces for analysis/discernment. They touch on some of the reasons that sustain and some of the reasons that negate the faith conviction and the sense of benefit upon which this collaboration rests. Transformation of SCUPE has already begun. Like most transformations, it has realities that it did not choose, but also choices and the potential for new programs that would call for celebration and give new status to different partners. If the goal of the program is to keep seminaries invested in training urban ministers, then at this point that goal may be better served by assisting in the insertion of the urban dimension and the process of education that have evolved from it into the locus of theological schools. SCUPE may have to go where adult learners are in order to educate the schools themselves. Consultations that allow SCUPE to collaborate in helping each school to discern/analyze its institutional vocation would be an effective way of sharing the fruits of SCUPE's trustworthy struggle to learn how to learn and act in ways that foster the city's realization of God's reign and how to incorporate these learnings into the curriculum.

Collaboration with ATS and the seminaries who are committed

to the shalom of the city might yield ways to keep supporting urban ministers without their first academic degree in their journey to accredited professional education. New York Seminary and CUME, for instance, both have long track records and much wisdom that may be fruitfully translated into SCUPE's and Chicago's realities. Urban ministry cannot flourish if it is isolated from larger society. Higher education, especially colleges and universities with urban locations, have become invested in the wellness of the city, building bridges on which the traffic flows in both ways. Many service, intern, and volunteer programs send undergraduate and graduate students into the heart of the city. Reflective and interdisciplinary analysis and discernment in experienced-based learning are new crafts for traditional academics, including those in seminaries. SCUPE has much to share in this area. Collaboration with urban partners is also inviting them into the university.

The Center for Urban Research and Learning at Loyola University in Chicago, to cite but one example, is a new form of collaboration. CURL is a multi-disciplinary center that works with community-based groups to provide the research that these groups request and to work with them in producing it. Together they have developed such things as a participatory evaluation program for a health center and gathered solid data about the impact of city, state, and federal policy and legislative changes on housing, health, and food programs. They are answering questions that the community organizations, not the academic, ask. CURL has also generated a foundation database, giving NPOs (nonprofit organizations) access to it and providing training for grant writers and foundation officers.

As these educational relationships shift, they still need the discerning analysis and insight of experienced programs like SCUPE. Conferences, consultations, and written material all seem fairly rare in this area of education. My basic response is to want to celebrate and affirm all that SCUPE has achieved in its pursuit of its vocation, and to ask it to accept its freedom to do this differently. Its discernment/analysis will require continuing collaboration and readiness to be open to the transformation — or even death — of the present program. The vocation of SCUPE, the integrity and effectiveness of its realization of this vocation, has power. Choose wisely!

The case from Metro Strategy seems to ask: How can Metro Strategy expand its faith community membership? It is exciting to see the churches of this area reach out to the resources developed and tested over time by agencies for change that have no church affiliation. As some of my reflections above indicate, I regret that I cannot find a deeper integration of the superb theological assumptions of Metro Strategy and the effective technical training of IAF. Who will deal with those who object to IAF's method and style? Who will minister to those who are resisting change, with those so shaped by the kinds of prejudices that appear so blatantly in some of the statements of St. Mary's members? If St. Mary's decides not to join Metro Strategy, will that be the end of Metro Strategy's outreach to them — or does Metro Strategy apply its vision of church to itself — and how?

It seems to me that a "pre-evangelization" might be helpful in approaching new members. Friendship and respect for Father Michael are not enough to give Father John the confidence and resources needed to examine his own beliefs and to be able to understand the newer developments in theological thought so that he and his parish may be more aware of the ways in which new life might come to them and through them. Perhaps Metro Strategy's own leadership is called to truly "own" the integration of its theological stances and the choice of action implicit in them and then to assist its present and potential faith community members to do the same. This will prepare them for what seems to me essential when they expand the faith communities included in their network beyond the Judeo-Christian tradition . . . assuming they will deal with this explicitly. There is no indication that Metro Strategy has addressed the different principles and assumptions that may be guiding its union or parent members. The more "privatized" the guiding convictions, the more fully will self-interest become the public and primary bond. Is that going to be life-giving for Metro Strategy? Will it produce inclusive and enduring membership?

Critical in both these cases, then, is the issue of collaboration: How will a community of partners be formed and maintained so that the goal of the city's shalom can be furthered by this group? The futures for both SCUPE and Metro Strategy seem to me bright — but not without some genuine transformations. Both of these programs have a developed faith stance and spirituality that is a God-based foundation for their understanding of and relationship to all that is, and this is more than abundant enough to nourish them on the journey.

III. PARADIGMS FOR URBAN TRANSFORMATION

ELDIN VILLAFAÑE

Tradition holds that as St. Peter was leaving Rome, the Lord confronted him with a piercing query — *Quo Vadis?* (Where are you going?). As we begin a new century and a new millennium, it is appropriate to raise this question again, this time addressing it to all responsible for theological education for urban ministry.

The programs presented in this book exemplify and are exemplary of the strength and the challenges facing urban theological education. These are distinct educational ministries that respond to the distinct and complex urban ethos of their respective *polis*. And yet, whether they are located in Boston, Chicago, New York City, Philadelphia, or Los Angeles, they ultimately represent contemporary disciples of Jesus committed to "Seek the *shalom* of the city" (Jer. 29:7). These disciples of Jesus and their examples of urban theological education are challenging the church and its theological institutions to respond to the problems and promises of our cities in a biblically and theologically relevant manner.

One can utilize our six frames of reference — contextualization, constituency, community, curriculum, collaboration, and confession — to highlight essential elements found in our cases that are crucial for the reframing of theological education for urban ministry. By subsuming these frames under the key hermeneutical frame of contextualization, I will underline some of the learnings and contributions for urban theological education and the challenges that must be faced. Thus, pro-

191

viding a provisional response to the question that must always be asked of any of the church's ministries — *Quo Vadis?*

Contextualization: The Key Hermeneutical Frame

Contextualization is the *sine qua non* of all faithful and effective urban theological education. All our examples see the city as a unique context demanding a distinctive response. The city is not only the *locus* of these programs; it is the *logos* of their educational ministry. As the predominant habitat of persons in our postmodern world, the city is both a *locus* and a complex of systems. The city as such challenges theological education to an incarnated presence *(locus)* and a discerning exegesis *(logos)* of its complex systems. Furthermore, the postmodern city challenges theological education to model an urban community *(koinonia)*.

The City as *Locus*

All the examples presented affirm the importance of *locus*. In the words of Michael Mata, they "take seriously the urban landscape where most of their students live, work and minister."[1] They recognize with Warren Dennis that "more than ever before, we are embarking on a new urban reality that expands the definition of urban to encompass a metro-urban character." In addition, "this metropolitan character of the merger of suburban-urban public policy, population, commerce, information technology, land-use, and governance calls for new curricular responses to preparation for urban ministry." Yet, our cases illustrate that contextualization may be best defined by the biblical paradigm of incarnation (John 1:14; Phil. 2:5-11). The leaders of the various programs outlined in the cases realize that while urban theological education is to serve the whole city — the neighborhoods as well as the greater metropolitan area — it begins with and contextually expresses a commitment to and solidarity with those with whom Jesus did. In the language of Leonardo Boff or Gustavo Gutiérrez, it manifests "a prefer-

---

1. The persons cited in this essay, unless otherwise noted, are the authors of the case commentaries contained in this volume.

ential option for the poor." Indeed, urban theological education is challenged to humbly express an "urban *kenosis*." It must struggle to empty itself of the prerogatives of power and prestige so highly valued by academia and the world, and pitch its tent among the poor and marginalized communities in our cities.[2] As these examples of urban theological education have learned well, redemptive ministry in the city demands incarnation, and its logical consequence — the cross.

Contextualization for Haggard Graduate School of Theology means situating its Urban Center in South Central L.A. Yet, some serious questions and concerns emerge. Michael Mata notes, "when does an institution that sees itself as taking its resources 'into' the city become part of the urban context? There are real differences in providing education 'to, in, and with.' This raises a significant issue in regard to the meaning and process of contextualization."

For Haggard's Urban Center, contextualization also means to struggle with a decontextualized faculty, one in need of urban "lived" experience and ministry — a faculty that is summoned, in the words of one of its students, "to engage the life of the city . . . who understand our world, who help us interpret the gospel to our people and transform our communities."

Contextualization has taken many forms for New York Theological Seminary. It has sought to serve the city by missiological, structural, theological, and pedagogical contextualization. Yet it is challenged once again to respond to a unique *locus,* one that sadly claims the life of inordinate numbers of African Americans and Latinos — Sing Sing Prison.

Carolyn Tennant's challenge to academia regarding its response to the changing urban *locus* is both insightful and pertinent:

> Our academic world can become too comfortable, too predictable: a kind of virtual reality shooting gallery in which we respond within a computer-generated space, acting as if it is reality. In this environment, we can trip over things, jerk in response, move forward or backward. There's just one problem. It's not the real world.

2. Eldin Villafañe, "A Prayer for the City: Paul's Benediction and a Vision for Urban Theological Education," *CONTACT* 28, no. 2 (Fall 1998): 14.

At the heart of contextualization, and any reframing of theological education for urban ministry for that matter, are the vision, faith, and commitment to move beyond our "comfort zone" into places *(loci)* pregnant with redemptive possibilities and hope.

The City as *Logos*

The city as *logos* speaks to the need to analyze the complex systems that make up the city. For example, System Thinking has been for the past few years a focal point of the Center for Urban Ministerial Education's (CUME) doctoral ministry program and its core courses in urban ministry. As such, it has begun to offer students another powerful tool for understanding the city.

The city as *logos* means above all that the theology of urban *theological* education must be informed by serious biblical reflection and Spirit-led discernment of its context — thus, the city as *locus theologicus*. The theological assumptions and teachings about the city *per se* are vital to any educational endeavor. How one sees the city — its people, its web of institutions and power — will influence educational policy, programmatic and curricula development, and relational commitments. It will ultimately determine a missiological thrust that is either domesticating or liberating.

While most of our examples underline the teaching of social analysis of urban socio-political systems (e.g., NYTS, CUTS, CUME), it is the Seminary Consortium for Urban Pastoral Education (SCUPE) that has articulated and institutionalized the added theological-ethical analysis of "principalities and powers" as a framing theological perspective of its program.

The understanding of the "powers" is crucial for any theology of the city — indeed, for seeking justice and the *shalom* of the city! For the city, it is sad to note, in the language of the "powers," is increasingly becoming a "configuration of death." That is, the complex configuration of social living brought about by such urban systems and institutions as family, school, commerce, media, politics, culture, and religion are under the power of death. These systems or institutions that make up the city must be challenged to fulfill their God-given mission (vocation). As Max Stackhouse states, "it is not only a political duty to sus-

194

tain a context in which social institutions may be formed to guide the powers, it becomes a theological responsibility of academia and ecclesia to expose their spiritual pretensions, and to convert them into forces that serve the larger vision."[3]

The city as a "dominion" — a unique cultural and societal pattern in a particular region — must not only be socially and theologically analyzed and discerned; it must be confronted with the liberating gospel of our Lord. Only then will the city fulfill its mission (vocation) to establish "order" and conditions of "quality of life" for all its people.

Contextualization challenges all endeavoring to prepare a leadership for the city with a theological-ethical understanding of the "principalities and powers," resulting in a discerning exegesis *(logos)* of the city's complex system.

The city as *logos* also speaks to the challenges of curriculum being formed and informed by the community. The urban curriculum, in the words of Richard White, must "be allowed to reflect the culture, social fabric, and religious ethos of the community in which it is embedded." This raises many questions. Does the curriculum respond to the changing constituency of our cities? More specifically, does the curriculum serve the multiracial, multiethnic, multicultural, and increasingly multilingual reality of our cities? For example, CUME from its inception has taught courses in English and Spanish, and has added through the years a curriculum program in Portuguese (serving the Brazilian community), French Creole (for the Haitian community), and American Sign Language (for the deaf community). New York Theological Seminary serves its constituency in English, Spanish, and Korean.

What about the question of pedagogical/andragogical contextualization? Does learning tailored to the adult learner prevail in our urban examples, thus andragogy (teaching adults)? Or is the curriculum captive to the pedagogy (teaching children) of the academy, that, in the words of Leah Gaskin Fitchue, is a "prison of abstraction?" Roger Greenway would remind us that andragogy "is the most effective way to teach adults, especially highly motivated adults such as those enrolled at CUTS and CUME." He further reminds us of the need to overcome

---

3. Max L. Stackhouse, "Globalization, Faith, and Theological Education," *Theological Education* 35, no. 2 (Spring 1999): 74; see especially his section, "Power, Authorities, Thrones and Dominions," pp. 72-76.

the dissonance (Richard White would call it "reduction of curriculum/ community mismatch") with the "pedagogical methods [that] predominate among schools connected to the 'academy' . . . [and] the expectations of traditional accrediting associations."

Urban theological education is challenged to develop non-traditional academic approaches and alternative educational methodologies and styles, ones that are appropriate to the mostly adult learners they serve, and to the multicultural, multilingual, multiracial, and multiethnic realities in which they work. This may include, among other things: student-centered vocational enrichment and remedial courses, English as a Second Language (ESL), a predominance of evening classes, flexible degree programs, multilingual course offerings, and the use of computers and cross-cultural video and written sources. Urban theological programs should strengthen and highlight the use of mentors drawn from the community. Experienced local lay and clergy leaders have both the power and potential to be invaluable mentors and colleagues who join students as partners or companions in disciplined reflection to explore issues of faith.

All our cases understand the importance of a curriculum that builds socio-theological capital. They know, with Richard White, that "theological education introduces students to the concepts and tools that allow them to think critically and act with confidence in ministry." This leads to the purpose of building socio-theological capital and the objectives of urban theological education, namely:

> (1) to *form* pastors and teachers and other leaders among the people of God; (2) to *inform* them about the Scripture, tradition, reason, and experience in social, cultural, and concrete historical contexts; so that (3) they may serve as agents of *transformation* in the churches, denominations, and social communities in which God has placed them.[4]

The task of engaging in "transforming education" requires the development of skills vital to the public life and civic responsibility of

---

4. Eldin Villafañe, *Seek the Peace of the City: Reflections on Urban Ministry* (Grand Rapids: Eerdmans, 1995), p. 84; and "New Alternatives for Theological Education," *Fraternidad Teológica Latinoamericana*, Quito, Ecuador, 1985, mimeograph, p. 9.

the urban church. Programmatic tools of transformation are skills of theological and social analysis, congregational and community organization, community development, civic and social spirituality, and multicultural community conflict resolution.

The city is a place of concentrated community conflict. My co-authors Alice and Bob Evans have argued in *Peace Skills: A Manual for Community Mediators*[5] that conflict is dangerous and destructive, as was clearly demonstrated in urban uprisings such as those in Los Angeles, Cincinnati, and other U.S. cities. However, as urban ministry leaders know, conflict also provides opportunities for systemic change. Faithful ministry preparation provides skill training and theological insight for transforming situations by empowering people to move toward reconciliation with justice. Conflict transformation goes beyond conflict resolution and management to structural change. Seminaries and urban ministry programs need to provide spiritual, moral, and cultural resources for systemic peacebuilding. In addition, these institutions and the lives of faculty members and mentors must also model the patterns of renewal and reconciliation mandated in the biblical call to be agents of reconciliation (2 Corinthians 5).

All our cases agree that if we are to provide for a liberating educational paradigm, and seriously impact our urban context, our curriculum must go beyond the "classical disciplines" of the academy to develop action-reflection approaches that are epistemologically sound and socially relevant.

The City as *Koinonia*

The postmodern city challenges both the church and urban theological education to commit to a wholistic urban *koinonia*. In Scripture, particularly in Pauline writings, *koinonia* is a rich and fruitful word-concept yielding multiple meanings. It can mean fellowship or communion with, or participation in something, as well as collaboration, sharing,

5. Alice Frazer Evans, Robert A. Evans, and Ronald S. Kraybill, *Peace Skills: A Manual for Community Mediators;* and *Peace Skills: Leader's Guide* (San Francisco: Jossey Bass Publishers, 2000).

giving, distribution, and partnership.[6] It speaks to us of solidarity and community. In biblical Christianity *koinonia* is a mark of maturity — of true spirituality.

Urban theological education gives witness to this *koinonia* to the extent that its life and mission are informed by and demonstrate authentic partnership or collaboration. All our examples give witness to an urban *koinonia*. They have learned that "the 'Lone Ranger' mentality of ministry in the city reflects not only poor stewardship of our God-given resources, but a crass and ultimately counterproductive vision of service."[7] They have also learned early in their ministry that urban theological education requires a sustained and sustainable spiritual, moral, and funding base rooted in partnerships.

Of all our examples, SCUPE, by virtue of its structure as a consortium, has had the greatest challenge in maintaining that healthy and creative tension that defines collaborative educational ventures. Applying the words of Mary Hennessey, SCUPE has affirmed and kept before its partners "the importance and rightness of working together AND the awareness that, in working together, there will be benefits that could never be achieved singly."

The Los Angeles Metro-Strategy challenges both the local parish and all urban theological education programs to an enlarged vision of collaboration — of *koinonia*. The city as *koinonia*, if anything, speaks to a collaboration that is as *large* as the city, as *wide* as the programs servicing it, and as *deep* as its confessional representatives. In the interest of serving the city as agents of justice and *shalom*, an urban *koinonia* must be demonstrated that transcends the parochial interest of individual seminaries, churches, denominations, or religious traditions.

This presents a great challenge to our urban theological programs and institutions, which should, nay *must*, be in collaboration with the many and diverse: neighborhoods or communities of service; congregations and faith traditions dotting our cities; grassroots parachurch organizations and service agencies; municipal institutions; and public and private delivery systems in our cities. The *shalom* of our cities de-

---

6. C. K. Barrett, *A Commentary on the Second Epistle to the Corinthians* (New York: Harper & Row, 1973), p. 345.

7. Villafañe, "A Prayer for the City," p. 21.

mands from all its benevolent actors no more and no less than this kind of wholistic *koinonia* — in truth, an authentic spirituality.

The challenges of reframing theological education for urban ministry are many. The emerging frames presented in this book are an interpretive approach to the task before us. They should serve us well in how we view urban ministry in general and urban theological education in particular. They should be helpful for the journey before us, and for a faithful response to the Lord's *Quo Vadis?*

Authors and Contributors

Authors

Alice Frazer Evans is director of writing and research, Plowshares Institute; Senior Fellow, Centre for Conflict Resolution at the University of Cape Town, South Africa; and adjunct faculty, Hartford Seminary. Her work in equipping religious and civic leaders to deal constructively with community conflict has involved extensive programs in Africa, Asia, and North America. She co-directed with Robert Evans a ten-year program titled Globalization of Theological Education with twelve North American theological seminaries. She is the co-director emeritus of the Association for Case Teaching, the author of numerous national and international case studies, and the editor, author, and/or co-author of a dozen case books including *Christian Ethics: A Case Method Approach; The Globalization of Theological Education,* and *Peace Skills,* a manual and curriculum for community mediators. She is an ordained elder in the Presbyterian Church, serving on the governing board of an inner-city congregation in Hartford. She was educated at Agnes Scott College, the University of Edinburgh, and the University of Wisconsin.

Robert A. Evans is the founding executive director of Plowshares Institute, which is committed to education, research, and dialogue for a more just, sustainable, and peaceful world community. He studied at the Universities of Yale, Edinburgh, and Basel, and earned his doctorate from Union Theological Seminary (New York). An ordained Presbyterian pastor, he served pastorates in urban and suburban congregations, and as a professor in seminaries and universities in New York, Chicago, Uganda, Fiji, and Hartford. He currently serves as a Senior Fellow, Centre for Conflict Resolution at the University of Cape Town. He co-directed with Alice Frazer Evans a pilot program with religious leaders in Philadelphia and Los Angeles that eventually expanded to eight other North American cities, and he equips multiethnic teams of religious and civic leaders to be proactive interveners in community conflict situations. The Evanses are currently developing programs in conflict transformation and sustainable development in Timor Lorosae (formerly East Timor), Hong Kong, Indonesia, Kenya, Uganda, and Zimbabwe. He is the author, co-author, and/or editor of a dozen books, including *Pedagogies for the Non-Poor; Human Rights: A Dialogue between the First and Third Worlds;* and *Peace Skills for Community Mediators.*

Bruce W. Jackson, as assistant dean of Gordon-Conwell Theological Seminary (Boston campus), helps oversee the programs of CUME and coordinates the Doctor of Ministry track, "Ministry in Complex Urban Settings." As an assistant professor of Christian Education and Urban Ministry, he teaches in the areas of Christian education, church administration and management, research, critical thinking, urban ministry, and systems thinking. His doctorate in education is from Boston University. He served as the program director of the Contextualized Urban Theological Education Program (CUTEP), a national re-granting program sponsored by the Pew Charitable Trusts to encourage the formation of partnerships in urban theological education. He was a founding member of New Life Fellowship Baptist Church, Allston, Massachusetts, where he was ordained to the gospel ministry. He has ministered in India, New Zealand, Kenya, and Mexico, focusing on urban theological education. He is secretary of the Association for Urban Theological Education and Ministry (AUTEM) and the recording secretary for Urban Theologians International. He is an active member of the North American Professors of Christian Education (NAPCE).

Eldin Villafañe is the Ricardo Tañon Distinguished Professor of Hispanic Christianity, Ethics, and Urban Ministry at Gordon-Conwell Theological Seminary and the president of the Asociación para la Educación Teológica Hispana (AETH). His doctorate was awarded by

Boston University. Dr. Villafañe was the founding director (1976-90) of the Center for Urban Ministerial Education (CUME) and former Associate Dean of Urban and Multicultural Affairs at Gordon-Conwell Theological Seminary. He served as the first president of La Comunidad of Hispanic American Scholars of Theology and Religion, and was the former president of the Society for Pentecostal Studies (SPS). He is an ordained minister of the Assemblies of God, Spanish Eastern District, and has been named one of the nation's ten most influential Hispanic religious leaders and scholars by the *National Catholic Reporter*. He is the author of *The Liberating Spirit: Toward an Hispanic American Pentecostal Social Ethic; Seek the Peace of the City: Reflections on Urban Ministry;* and *A Prayer for the City: Further Reflections on Urban Ministry*. Dr. Villafañe was a visiting professor at Harvard Divinity School in the fall of 1998. He was the second person to occupy the recently established Luce lectureship in Urban Ministry.

Contributors

Warren L. Dennis is ordained in the Presbyterian Church (USA) and is associate professor and director of metro-urban ministry at New Brunswick Theological Seminary, New Brunswick, New Jersey. He is vice president of the Association for Urban Theological Education and Ministry (AUTEM). He earned the M.Div. from Johnson C. Smith Seminary in Atlanta, and D.Min. from United Theological Seminary, Dayton, Ohio. He has special interest in examining issues of poverty, race, and culture in urban theological education.

Leah Gaskin Fitchue is president of The Gaskin Fitchue Group, which provides faith-based consultation for churches, community organizations, and seminaries. She has served as an associate professor and director of urban ministry programs at Eastern Baptist Theological Seminary and as a mentor for Doctor of Ministry students at United Theological Seminary. She currently works with the Transpacific Alliance for Urban Theological Education and is a member of the national steering committee of the Association of Urban Theological Education and Ministry (AUTEM). An Itinerant Elder of the African Methodist Episcopal Church, she has served as an Associate Pastor in urban

202

churches in New Jersey and Pennsylvania. She is a graduate of Douglass College of Rutgers University, University of Michigan, Princeton Theological Seminary, and received her doctorate from Harvard University. Her publications include: "Breaking the Silence," in *Women of Color Study Bible* and "Head, Heart and Hands: Black Theology as a Source of Empowerment," in "What Does It Mean to Be Black and Christian?" in *Pulpit, Pew, and Academy in Dialogue,* vol. 2.

Robert M. Franklin is president of the Atlanta-based Interdenominational Theological Center, a historical national center of African-American religious training and graduate education. He is a graduate of Morehouse College and of Harvard University, and received his doctorate from the University of Chicago. Prior to assuming the presidency of the ITC, he was a program officer at the Ford Foundation. He has taught at Harvard Divinity School, Colgate-Rochester Divinity School, and Candler School of Theology at Emory University. He is the author of *Another Day's Journey: Black Churches Confronting the American Crisis,* in which he urges an activist Christian commitment by churches to resolving America's mounting social problems; and *Liberating Visions: Human Fulfillment and Social Justice in African American Thought.*

David J. Frenchak is president of the Seminary Consortium for Urban Pastoral Education (SCUPE) in Chicago and a Fellow of the Case Method Institute. He has co-edited two books on urban ministry, *Metro Ministry: Ways and Means of the Urban Church* and *Signs of the Kingdom in the Secular City,* and has authored a number of articles. He is a father of two, an adjunct seminary professor, and a former urban pastor in Boston, Massachusetts. He received an M.Div. degree from Bethel Theological Seminary and holds a D.Min. degree from Andover Newton Theological School. He and his wife, Carol Ann McGibbon, are restoring a Victorian home in Chicago.

Roger S. Greenway is professor of world missiology at Calvin Theological Seminary in Grand Rapids, Michigan. He previously served his denomination as Executive Director of Christian Reformed World Ministries. He taught urban missions at Westminster Theological Seminary in Philadelphia, and was the founding editor of the journal *Urban Mission.* As a missionary of the Christian Reformed Church, he served in Sri

Lanka, Mexico, and other parts of Latin America. He is currently on the pastoral staff of an inner-city church in Grand Rapids. He holds a Th.M. degree from Calvin Seminary and a Th.D. from Southwestern Baptist Theological Seminary. He is the author and/or editor of more than a dozen books, several of which have been translated and published in other languages. His books include: *Apostles to the City; Discipling the City; Cities: Missions' New Frontier;* and *Go and Make Disciples.*

Youtha Hardman-Cromwell is the associate director of the Practice in Ministry and Mission Program at Wesley Theological Seminary in Washington, D.C. She is an elder in the Virginia Conference of the United Methodist Church and previously gave leadership to the Ford Field-Based Fellowship Program at Howard University School of Divinity. She pastored Woodlawn United Methodist Church, Alexandria, Virginia, from 1986 to 1989. She has a Ph.D. in Education Administration from American University and an M.Div. from Howard University School of Divinity. As dramatist for Youth and Friends, she presents God's Trombones with Negro Spirituals for churches and other organizations. She and her husband Oliver have four adult children and one granddaughter.

Mary Hennessey has served on the faculties of the Institute of Pastoral Studies of Loyola University, Chicago; St. Mary's Seminary and University, Baltimore; and Harvard Divinity School in the areas of ministerial studies and theological field education. Her urban ministry has been primarily with women and children without homes, the imprisoned, those living with HIV/AIDS, and those who are working with them in both systemic and pastoral ways. She is a member of the Cenacle, an international community of Roman Catholic sisters whose focus is on supporting the awakening and deepening of faith and the living out of right relationships with all creation in the whole human family.

Michael Mata is director of the Urban Leadership Institute and teaches urban ministry courses at the Claremont School of Theology. He is also chairperson of the Christians Empowering for Reconciliation with Justice group in Los Angeles and has been part of a two-year community conflict transformation training program with Plowshares Institute. He is known in the community as a consummate networker and crafter of coalitions, particularly among religious groups. He was extensively involved in the rebuilding efforts after the 1992 Los Angeles riots, helping to organize the African-American, Latino, and Korean evangelical leadership.

Anne Reissner, former academic dean of the Maryknoll School of Theology, is the Director of Study for the Center for Mission Research and Study at Maryknoll. She holds a D.Min. degree and M.Div. degree from Andover Newton Theological School, Newton, Massachusetts, and an M.R.E. degree from LaSalle College, Pennsylvania. She has served as president of the Association for Case Teaching and is currently a member of the Board of Advisors for that Association. Her publications include several case studies that have been published in the *Journal for Case Teaching* as well as numerous articles on using case method in teaching theology. She is a founding member and chair of the Board of Directors for the not-for-profit organization Hudson Link for Higher Education in Prison, which seeks to provide college programs for persons incarcerated in Sing Sing Prison.

Carolyn Tennant is the vice president for academic affairs at North Central University in Minneapolis. Located in the urban center since 1930, North Central is a forerunner in the development of an undergraduate program in Urban Ministries. Through a grant by the Pew Charitable Trusts, North Central University's City Gate project has been the hub of a cooperative effort among Twin Cities seminaries and schools to offer a full array of urban curriculum from the institute through the seminary venues. Besides being a driving force in the development of these urban programs, she is leading curriculum change in her university to connect with our society. She holds a Ph.D. from the University of Colorado and is ordained in the Assemblies of God. She has an active speaking schedule across the U.S. and in other countries.

Mark S. R. Walden is coordinator of marketing and development for the Seminary Consortium for Urban Pastoral Ministry (SCUPE) in Chicago and an adjunct instructor at Morton College in Cicero, Illinois. He was previously a Charles Finney Fellow with Evangelicals for Social Action. Mark earned an M.A. from Eastern Baptist Theological Seminary and has written for *Sojourners* magazine and other publications. He has extensive experience in assisting diverse U.S. and international students in research projects and in planning and writing papers. He and his wife Julie live in Oak Park, Illinois, and are part of a Chicago house church.

Richard White is the executive director of Contextualized Urban Ministry Education Northwest and an adjunct professor of community studies at Portland State University. He was bi-vocational for much of the twenty years he served as pastor in Christian Church congregations. He has ministered in and with low-income and ethnic communities in central California, the Appalachians of North Carolina, and inner-urban Portland, Oregon. He has also worked in the field of community development as an organizer and project manager. In the late 1960s at San Jose Christian College, he developed an interest in urban and non-traditional ministries. He received his M.Div. from Emmanuel School of Religion and the Ph.D. in urban studies from Portland State University.

Sue Zabel is associate professor and Director, Practice in Ministry and Mission at Wesley Theological Seminary in Washington, D.C. and a field consultant with The Alban Institute, Bethesda, Maryland. She is the chairperson of the Association for Theological Field Education and past president of the Association for Case Teaching. She holds a Ph.D. from the University of Minnesota, a Master of Science in Organizational Development from Pepperdine University, and a Master of Divinity from United Theological Seminary of the Twin Cities. She and her husband Alan are parents of three adult children and grandparents of one "unbelievably wonderful grandson."